D1601192

The
Waning
of the
Welfare
State

The Waning of the Welfare State

The End of Comprehensive State Succor

Anton C. Zijderveld

Transaction Publishers
New Brunswick (U.S.A.) and London (U.K.)

This book is printed on acid-free paper that meets the American National Standard for Permanence of Paper for Printed Library Materials.

Library of Congress Catalog Number: 98-53726
ISBN: 1-56000-405-3
Printed in the United States of America

Library of Congress Cataloging-in-Publication Data

Zijderveld, Anton C., 1937–
    The waning of the welfare state : the end of comprehensive state succor
/ Anton C. Zijderveld.
        p. cm.
    Includes bibliographical references and index.
    ISBN 1-56000-405-3 (alk. paper)
1. Welfare state—History. 2. Europe, Western—Social policy. 3. Democracy—Europe, Western—History. 4. Civil society—Europe, Western—History. 5. Socialism—Europe, Western—History. 6. Conservatism—Europe, Western—History. 7. Liberalism—Europe, Western—History. I. Boyle, Richard, 1955–   . II. Lemaire, Donald. III. Series.
JC479.Z55   1999
361.6'5'094—dc21   98-53726
                                                                    CIP

For Susi Zijderveld Nap

Contents

Preface

The title of this book with its perhaps inexcusable yet to the author nonetheless enticing alliteration, is an obvious nod to Johan Huizinga's famous study of the late Burgundian Middle Ages. It does however stand in need of a brief explanation. The title should not be misread. The main argument of the book is *not* that the welfare state will or should disappear. *Waning* is meant as a fundamental transformation that makes room for renewal and regeneration. In fact, ever since Elizabeth I and her Poor Law, Western societies have held the state responsible for the care of the needy, the vulnerable and the weak; for the cure of the sick and the succor of the disabled. Thus, some form of state which is responsible for the well-being and welfare of its citizens, is and remains endemic to a society which aspires to be civilized. The question is, however, how extensive and intensive such a welfare state should be. It is argued in this book that the *comprehensive* (i.e., intensive and extensive) welfare state which most Western European countries have erected after the Second World War, has been reduced in both scope and intensity ever since roughly 1980.

In most postbellum countries of Western Europe, in which, incidentally, in this book Great Britain is included, the welfare state has been extended and intensified in a spectacular manner. In fact, the notion of "welfare" was broadened into a complex mix of services covering not just health, education and welfare, but the arts, leisure, and above all social security in the working place as well. It is the argument of this book that this comprehensive and well-nigh oceanic welfare state, which at times even seemed to pretend to secure the happiness of its citizens, has waned ever since the 1980s. We are heading, both in Europe and the United States, towards a more sober, much more decentralized and deregulated welfare state which takes care of its proper core business, i.e., being a constitutional state that secures safety and order to its citizens and offers a shield to the vulnerable in society. This leaner, meaner welfare state should leave sufficient space for the market to develop and for civil society to prosper. As the close of the century draws near and the dawn of the new millennium approaches we are experiencing in a sense a sort of cultural Renaissance, as well as a socioeconomic and political Reformation.

The focus of the book is Europe, but it is believed that the European welfare state experience of the past four decades is of interest to American readers who should weigh the advantages and disadvantages of these experiences. They will, it is hoped, discover beyond the vast differences, some basic similarities of structure and development, through a comparison of welfare state experiences in America and Europe.

The various arguments in this book concerning the basic transformations of the comprehensive welfare state of the 1960s and 1970s, are based upon a rather simple theoretical model, explained in more detail in the last chapter, yet briefly outlined at the outset. It is the notion of a *Democratic Triangle* in which democracy, whatever this concept may contain and entail, is viewed as a system in which State, Market, and (Civil) Society are held in precious balance. If one of these components supersedes the other two, democracy is endangered. These three components of the Democratic Triangle also represent the three main political ideologies of democracy: social democracy, liberalism, and conservatism (or, in some European countries, Christian democracy).

When the welfare state grows ever more comprehensive, the increasingly centralized state will become enlarged at the expense of the market and civil society. This is, of course, what happened *ad absurdum* in communism but, albeit still in terms of (an often somewhat shaky) democracy, in many Western European societies as well. The 1960s and 1970s, the true heyday of the comprehensive welfare state in Western Europe, witnessed the predominance of the state at the expense of the market and civil society. Social democracy, often crudely labeled socialism, was the predominant ideology. The 1980s were the decade in which the market "recaptured" its position in the Democratic Triangle, often at the expense of both the state and civil society. It was the decade of liberalism, often erroneously held to be "conservative." (Mrs. Thatcher and Mr. Reagan were in terms of socioeconomic policy true liberals, not conservatives!). The 1990s witness the "recovery" of civil society, which again runs the risk of being injurious to the position of the state and the market (as, for example, in *communitarianism*).

Ideologically, this is the decade of conservatism and a conservative view of the welfare state. However, the near future may well witness a fortuitous balance within the Democratic Triangle, and thus a basic coalition of social democracy, liberalism, and conservatism. This will be to the benefit of the state (i.e., to safety and order), to the market (i.e., to prosperity and economic participation), and to civil society (i.e., to social participation and meaningful interactions). Again, all of this will be discussed in more detail at the end of the book, but as it is the main focus of the arguments to follow, keep this in mind while reading the beginning chapters.

Portions of this book have appeared before in a Dutch publication which I wrote at the end of the 1970s, together with my colleague Hans P. Adriaansens of the University of Utrecht. I used only the chapters I myself authored but did much more than just translate them into English. A complete overhaul was necessary. Adriaansens's influences, however, were and still are considerable, particularly as far as horizontalism and verticalism as two structural principles are concerned. I am, however, responsible for the manner in which I incorporated these heuristically useful concepts in the present book.

I received valuable bibliographical assistance from Jacqueline Markvoort and Hennie Helmer, while Dick Houtman, senior research assistant at the Sociology Department of Erasmus University helped me by writing two extensive reviews of the relevant literature. I am grateful for these contributions but again remain solely responsible for their incorporation into the present arguments.

The project was financed by the Bradley Foundation through the Institute for the Study of Economic Culture (ISEC) of Boston University. It enabled me to stay in Boston at regular intervals, work in the library of Boston University and engage in the seminal discussions that are the core of ISEC. As always, the intellectual and personal support of ISEC's director Peter L. Berger and of Brigitte Berger were a veritable *conditio sine qua non* for this book.

I dedicate the book to my daughter Susanne M. Zijderveld Nap. She lives and works as a lawyer in Amsterdam, mainly in the field of medical care with a focus on the as of yet rare private medical services. This sector is still young and vulnerable in the Netherlands and demonstrates as in a laboratory setting the promises and problems of the waning of the Dutch comprehensive welfare state. Recently, the present left-of-center government initiated legislation to curb the emergence of private health care—allegedly because it would cause a dual system of care, favoring the well-to-do. The main reason, however, may well be the fact that in the end of the day the private system will be too strong a competitor to the public system. It is indicative that the Ministry of

Health is the only department that over the past years has grossly exceeded its spending budgets. Apparently, the shadow of the comprehensive welfare state is long and tenacious, particularly in the field of medical cure and care.

Rotterdam, September 1998

Introduction

Not 1968, as is often claimed by many representatives of the baby boomer generation who were then politically active, but 1989 has been a year that witnessed a true revolution comparable to 1789 and 1917. That is, except for one crucial variable: it was a velvet revolution, which by and large unfolded without violence. Apart from the Romanian dictator and his wife, no "kings" or "czars" and consorts were executed. No counterrevolutionaries were brought to trial and convicted. Occasional purges occurred, as in the former German Democratic Republic where, after the reunification, former communists were removed from important political and societal positions, often replaced, as in the case of university professors, by younger Germans from the *Länder* in Western Germany. But on the whole, the transition from a communist and totalitarian to a capitalist and democratic society occurred peacefully. In fact, the communist empire simply collapsed ingloriously. It did not explode. It just imploded under the weight of its bureaucratic inefficiency and economic planning failures. The implosion left a huge political, economic, social, and cultural vacuum, soon filled with atavistic sentiments and acts of nationalism and racism, with local wars, such as in Bosnia and Chechnya. Naturally, there were those also who kept yearning for the old days of communist rule, which at least offered and assured a degree of security. Till now, however, they have remained a negligible minority which is rather pitiful, particularly when they demonstrate in the Kremlin and praise Stalin as the allegedly much needed model of great statemanship. The tattered economy fostered a vigorous black market and attracted, of course, various forms of organized crime. For several reasons—one of them being the persistence of a tradition of civil society—most Central European nations, the Czech Republic primarily, managed to survive after the implosion, and erected a relatively successful democratic polity as well as a viable, capitalist market.

The impressive performance of *Solidarnosc* in the 1980s, the collapse of the Soviet imperium, the end of state control of the market, the regained political autonomy of Central and Eastern European countries, the fall of the Berlin Wall and the ensuing reunification of Germany, have indeed the ramifications of a true revolution, as they brought about in a relatively short time very basic changes in the political, economic, social, and cultural structure of these societies. The political, socioeconomic and sociocultural map of Europe changed in a manner no one had dreamed off or could have predicted prior to the 1980s. The cold war ended in 1989. Europe entered a new era—an era, as we by now know, which is in many respects a very hot one, filled with both grave dangers and exhilarating promises and chances.

Parallel Developments

Indeed, as is in the nature of revolutions, all these rapid and fundamental changes have brought about myriad insecurities, uncertainties, and risks, but carry simultaneously the seeds of a much better and brighter future. However, the focus of this book is not on these crucial and fascinating developments in Central and Eastern Europe. It rather concerns itself with a fundamental transformation that has occurred ever since roughly 1980 in Western Europe. Although this transformation is far less spectacular than the revolution of the communist world in Central and Eastern Europe, it does carry grave consequences for the economy, the polity, the society and the culture of the countries concerned. In a sense, this transformation runs parallel to the revolution in formerly communist societies. The revolution in Central and Eastern European societies and the transformation of Western European welfare states have in common that they have affected the precious balance between the state, civil society and the market. The state loses is controlling primacy, the market has to regain its freedom, and civil society stands in need of revitalization.

The core of the less spectacular turnaround in Western Europe is the waning of the welfare state, which in most cases has been a comprehensive (that is, intensive and extensive) phenomenon with a heavy and often cumbersome impact on the polity, the economy, the society, and the culture of the nations concerned far beyond its proper realm of welfare and social security. Some desire and thus predict the complete eclipse of the welfare state, others like myself believe that some sort of welfare state will survive the present turmoil, although it is hard to predict its size and impact. In any case, there are in Western Europe at the moment, even among staunch proponents of social democracy, very few defenders of an unaltered, extensive and intensive welfare state.

This in itself is remarkable, since less than two decades ago critics of the welfare state were usually denounced as undesirable conservatives, if not reactionaries, while its social democratic or otherwise "progressive" advocates dominated both the policies of and the debates about the welfare state. In particular, members of the so-called New Class, or Knowledge Class, the intellectual, professional, and bureaucratic vanguard of the intensive and extensive welfare state (civil servants, welfare professionals, and social scientists) were able to set the agenda, and thus to defend successfully their own, particular interests.

Comprehensiveness: 1960–80

The idea and practice of a political administration responsible for the welfare of its citizens has, as we shall see in the next chapter, a relatively long history in Europe. But the welfare state—which tries to cover not just the social security of its citizens, insuring them against risks beyond their control, but also their economic, social and even psychological well-being, all of which is also seen as a package of social rights, and as a completion of democratic citizenship—is a relatively recent and geographically restricted phenomenon. Such a *comprehensive*, *intensive,* and *extensive*—in this sense, *total*—welfare state, dominating the market, the society, the polity, and the culture, penetrating deeply into the lives of individual citizens, emerged in most Western European countries after roughly 1960, and was transformed again rather radically after roughly 1980. Its heyday thus lasted but two decades. They have been exceedingly influential decades however.

There are, of course, scores of differences among the various European welfare states. But the largest difference has always been between these European welfare states and the welfare state to which most of the states of America have grown accustomed. Ever since Roosevelt's New Deal and Johnson's Great Society, the idea of a comprehensive welfare state has been fiercely contested, not in the least by the representatives of the Republican party. In fact, unlike most Europeans in the 1960s and 1970s, the majority of Americans has never been in favor of a comprehensive welfare state, as they are generally averse to a government which is too strongly centralized and too regulatory. A welfare state like the one in Sweden or the Netherlands (prior to the 1980s) is seen and abhorred by them as a semi-totalitarian system that subjects citizens to welfare dependence and gravely impairs their fundamental liberties.

Admittedly, this is an exaggeration, since Sweden and the Netherlands possess a strong democratic tradition in the context of a relatively vital civil society which fosters a basic consensus between labor and capital, state and citizens, contrary to what usually happens in totalitarian systems. Sweden also stands out within the European context by its focus on participation in the labor market. Social security in Sweden has never been a state-provided substitution for failing income, has never been a free ticket for the dole. On the contrary, it is meant to foster the reentry of recipients in the labor market. There remains much to be criticized in the Swedish welfare state system (which, incidentally, is also undergoing a very drastic revision these days) but upon closer scrutiny it cannot by any stretch of the imagination be called a totalitarian system that fosters an ethos of apathy and loitering.

The fact remains that most Americans are reluctant to condone an intensive and extensive welfare state. Compared to most European specimens the American welfare state often appears rudimentary. But even here reductions in state-provided welfare services have set in after roughly 1980 during the Reagan administration, and has been continued by the succeeding administrations, including the present Democratic one. This welfare reform resembles in degree, speed and kind the transformation of the welfare state in Western European countries. For that reason, it might be worthwhile for the American reader to consider the various ramifications of this transformation of European welfare states, as they may well highlight some very fundamental socioeconomic, sociocultural, and political processes as seen through a magnifying glass.

Theories of convergence are to be approached with care and suspicion. Still the present reductions of the encompassing welfare state seem to bring Europe closer to America sociopolitically and socioeconomically. This convergence is, incidentally, not to the satisfaction of many Europeans who are under the very generalized impression that "American Capitalism" lacks social consciousness and conscience.[1] Being used to the comprehensive welfare state of the 1960s and 1970s many Europeans believe that there is in America not much of a welfare state to speak of. As a result, in left-of-center circles in particular the present transformation of the welfare state in Europe has been decried as deplorable and undesirable "Americanization." As often happens, when Europeans talk and write about the United States critically, they fail to take into consideration its perplexing diversity and pluriformity. In this case, they particularly fail to realize that there are among the various states of America remarkable differences of intensity and extension of statutory welfare provisions. Massachusetts, for one, harbors welfare state arrangements which can certainly compete with most welfare states in Western Europe.

In any case, since roughly 1980 Western Europe entered a new and crucial phase of development. Its economic, political and, although at a slower pace, social integration has gained momentum. The European Union developed into an economically, but ultimately also politically influential block—an increasingly powerful partner and competitor of North America and Asian capitalist nations, Japan in the first place. Simultaneously, its member states began to reconstruct and redirect their socioeconomic policies, culminating in a drastic transformation of the comprehensive welfare state. Decentralization, deconcentration, privatization, deregulation, and concomitant attempts to revitalize the market and civil society began after roughly 1980, and have held the 1990s in their firm grip. The process will undoubtedly continue into the next decade.

A Tragic Evolution

There is in the eyes of the beholder actually an element of tragedy in the welfare state. If one defines tragedy as the frustration of well-meant efforts and endeavors, the results of which are the very opposite of what one intended to bring about, the welfare state is inherently tragic. With the poverty of the nineteenth century and the Great Depression of the late 1920s in mind, it meant to put an end to the miseries of poverty, unemployment, bad housing, illiteracy, insufficient medical care, and a miserable old age, particularly among society's lower strata. But the more the welfare state matured, the more it developed into a solidly middle-class system which catered to the interests of very specific categories of people, civil servants, professionals, and socio-scientific members of the Knowledge Class. There also seems to be an intrinsic drive to expand the span of influence of the welfare state. The more intensive and extensive it grew, the more it seemed to affect in a negative manner the vitality and flexibility of both the market and civil society. These unintended, but nevertheless adverse developments in the end even threatened to undermine the essence of democracy because, in Tocquevillean terms, the equality which the welfare state tried to bring about eventually threatened even the most basic democratic liberties.

Cultural and Moral Dimensions

Apart from a few states, America managed to stay clear of this tragic intensity and extension of the European welfare states. However, during the 1980s even here the awareness grew that the centralized and regulating as well as regulated welfare state had become economically unsustainable and morally undesirable. It is against this background that this book should be read. It focuses on what lessons can be learned from the European experience with encompassing welfare states which for political, moral, and economic reasons had to turn around rather radically in the 1980s and 1990s. This book, it should be emphasized, does not intend to give a detailed historical reconstruction of the birth, spectacular rise, and equally spectacular decline of the intensive and extensive welfare state in Western Europe, nor will it engage in detailed comparisons of the various European cases. The book was written by a generalist, not a specialist. Moreover, the prime focus is not on the dimensions of economics and public policy, as is the case in most present-day studies on welfare state alterations, but rather on the *cultural and moral dimensions of the welfare state* and its impact on the market and civil society. It is my contention that this dimension has been underexposed in the bulk of literature about the welfare state.

Each socio-scientific argument is based upon and starts from a limited amount of premises, or, if you want, biases which are rarely revealed in advance. They usually emerge during the argument, and are then brought to light as well-nigh inevitable conclusions. These premises are predominantly of a normative nature and certainly not value-free or objective, as one is often made to believe. On the contrary, they usually play a strategic role in the selection and interpretation of allegedly "hard" data. It is, I think, a matter of fairness, if not honesty, to admit and mention one's presuppositions briefly in advance, even though one thereby makes oneself rather vulnerable. The greater part of the publications about the welfare state which I consulted in preparation of this book were written in the customary socio-scientific vein—filled with statistical data, charts, and graphs. The message apparently conveyed was that the interpretations and explanations given were not speculative but, on the contrary, based upon "hard" facts. Yet, even a superficially critical reading of these texts demonstrated in due course that data and facts were either arbitrarily selected or picked out to serve the political, usually left-of-center bias—or, as was usually the case, both. If, for example, a much cited book on "welfare capitalism" by a

Scandinavian social scientist, speaks about "illustrious Swedish socialists,"[2] claims that "Scandinavian social democracy was blessed [!] with a chronically divided right,"[3] and uses Marxists concept like "decommodification" the reader knows immediately that the statistical data presented have been selected and are being presented with but one goal in mind: singing the praises of the (preferably Scandinavian) comprehensive welfare state as the best of all possible worlds. Conservatism is adorned with adjectives like "authoritarian" and "paternalist";[4] its "etatist paternalism" is lumped together with "corporatism" which, the author claims in one breath, "found its greatest expression in Fascist ideology."[5]

In view of most social-democratic and neo-liberal (i.e., "progressive") analyses of the welfare state, the present one will probably be held to be conservative. I have some doubts about this qualification. For one, in real life I lean toward the "left-of-center" in socioeconomic matters, to the "right-of-center" as far as values and norms are concerned, and to the "center" when it comes to meaningful interactions within civil society. But I decided some time ago not to argue about this qualification, even if it is apparently used as a denunciation as is generally the case in socio-scientific circles. I prefer rather to start with a brief exposition of the premises or biases that lie at the root of the ensuing observations and arguments. There are four positive premises and one negative.

Basic Premises

As to the negative premise, it is *not* my intention to discuss the welfare state in terms of (in)equality and class structure. Consequently, power, obviously closely linked with class structure, is not a core issue here. These issues are certainly of great interest and importance but they have been dealt with extensively elsewhere. That, however, is not sufficient reason to underemphasize them here. More important is the fact that most analyses of the welfare state in terms of class, (in)equality, and power seem to be doomed to focus primarily on political and economic rather than cultural and moral issues. In fact, the main focus is on structures and processes in the state and the market at the expense of what happens in culture and civil society. If such analyses entertain in addition a left-of-center, "progressive" bias, as most of them do, there is usually a latent or even overt aversion to capitalism which is, however, nowadays generally accepted albeit grudgingly. Capitalism has

won, it is admitted, its worldwide battle with socialism and communism, but few left-of-center observers and analysts seem to be happy
with this victory and construct theories about two contrary types of
capitalism (Albert) or three (liberal, conservative, and social-democratic) worlds of capitalism (Esping-Andersen). It is doubtful if all this
helps us to gain a better understanding of the comprehensive welfare
state and its recent transformations.

The four positive premises of the present argument are in fact four
clusters, which will be explained in more detail in the ensuing discussion. First, like all socioeconomic, cultural, and political constructions
the welfare state is in essence a complex set of human actions and
interactions. Human behavior is viewed here first and foremost in terms
of meaningful interactions which occur at all times within the context
of institutionalized values and norms. It, therefore, is essentially a *moral
behavior*, even though it may express itself in amoralism or immoralism.
Second, even as a comprehensive system the welfare state was and is
meant to be rooted in democracy. Whatever else democracy is or ought
to be, its essence is viewed here in the active *participation* of citizens
in the *res publica*, particularly in their contribution to the production of
goods and services, either in terms of voluntarism or in terms of paid
labor, or both. When, for whatever reason, citizens are excluded from
this active participation democracy is at stake. Third, in a democracy
power is and ought to be legitimated power, that is, an influential force
that is somehow accepted by the participants of the democratic society.
In democracy power tries at all times and at all costs to become and
remain *authority,* which is power based upon conviction, acceptance,
voluntary compliance, and therefore not upon force or violence. In view
of the comprehensive welfare state and its transformations, not just
power but also authority is a crucial issue to discuss and analyze. Fourth,
although the original drive behind the erection of a welfare state was a
moral drive—the desire to never again experience the miseries of nineteenth-century poverty, and the deep social insecurity of the crisis of
the late 1920s of this century—it did develop rapidly into a massively
bureaucratized, functionally rational and thus *amoral system* of
redistribution with which it was increasingly difficult to identify emotionally. Reconstructions of or alternatives to the welfare state ought to
heed this element of *anomie* and alleviate it.

This is a theoretical book in that it is not a report of empirical research data, but rather an argument which chapter by chapter discusses
a remarkable phenomenon: the waning of the comprehensive welfare

state since roughly 1980. Moreover, unlike most analyses of the welfare state there is a strong emphasis upon the moral dimensions and foundations of this phenomenon. As to the secondary research data which I have used if I deemed them reliable, there are also other data which have shaped this book: my personal experiences as a citizen of a country which serves as a prime example of a comprehensive welfare state. Such experiential data are usually disregarded or concealed by academic social scientists, as they are deemed to be "subjective" and thus unreliable. However, if confronted systematically with comparative experiences from different nations and different societies, and if critically confronted with reliable secondary research data, such personal experiences, I am convinced, are heuristically very useful.

Basic Concepts

This book will not reproduce standard sociological theories and theorems. Nevertheless, a limited amount of sociological concepts—four of them, divided in two dilemmatic pairs—ought to be singled out here and explained in advance, since they are of crucial importance to the ensuing arguments. First, as rationalization and rationality stand at the theoretical core of the following analyses and arguments, the reader should bear in mind that there is an important and heuristically useful distinction, first made by Max Weber and next further elaborated by Karl Mannheim. It is the well-known distinction between *functional and substantial rationality*. Human behavior can be called functionally rational, if it focuses all attention and energy on the development and improvement of instruments, techniques, procedures—that is, means—to realize set goals, irrespective of their content and substance. If there are any values and norms involved in functional rationality, they could be called "efficiency" and "effectiveness." Beyond that functional rationality is in actuality fact value-free. However, the focus on means might be so dominant that people begin to believe that the means—the instruments, techniques, and procedures—are the very goals of their behavior and inner desires. It is a curious example of goal displacement, which is in many respects typical of a fully modernized society. In its final consequences, (functional) rationality turns (functionally) irrational.

Human behavior is substantially rational, if it is borne and driven by values and norms which enable actors to experience reality as a structured reality, the components and processes of which seem to hang together meaningfully. The substantially rational actor views and experiences reality as a *nomos* to which he relates in a cognitive and emotive mode.[6] Needless to add, substantial rationality is required in order to set the goals or aims to which functional rationality must relate in a sensible and productive manner. It is part of classical social theory to emphasize the weakening of substantial rationality in modernity which is caused by the spectacular rise of the functional rationality inherent in technology.

The second pair of concepts crucial to the present analysis of and argument about the welfare state is that of *organization and institution*, a distinction that runs parallel to the former one. Often the two concepts are confused and confounded. *Institution* is used here in the Durkheimean sense as a traditional pattern of behavior (of acting, thinking, and feeling) which is borne of values, norms, and meanings, and thus of substantial rationality. The predominant type of institutional influence is not "law" power but authority. The concept of *organization* refers to functional rationality, to the structuring of behavior in terms of specialized functions and power relations. If there are any values and norms at play here, it is those "thin" ones called efficiency and effectiveness. One should bear in mind that these are not essential and ontological, but dimensional and analytical concepts. The family, the school, the university, the church, the army, the labor union, the sporting club, etc., can and should be viewed simultaneously in terms of "institution" as well as "organization." If looked at and studied as an institution, we are interested in the history, the culture (the legends, myths, rituals) and the substantial rationality of a particular university. If approached and subjected to socio-scientific research as an organization, we will rather focus on the formal structure of power and command, on the dynamics of staff and line, on legal and financial formalities. The cultural-sociological approach as adopted in this book favors the institutional dimension. In fact, most analyses and interpretations of the welfare state have been conducted in terms of its organizational dimension, much to the detriment of its institutional dimension.

Defining the Welfare State

Meanwhile, the welfare state is and has been a very complex, multifaceted phenomenon, and there are substantial national differences to boot. As a result, the definitions of the welfare state are multiple, and so are the attempts to define its core, or essence. Needless to say, ideological preferences prevail when the welfare state is delineated conceptually. It makes a great deal of difference whether one views it as an instrument by which the working class is emancipated and socioeconomic inequalities are attacked, or rather as a universal social insurance providing all citizens with at least a minimum of social security as part of their constitutional rights and as an inalienable component of their citizenship. It also makes a difference whether one views the welfare state primarily as a financial and fiscal device through which to redistribute wealth, or rather as the legal and financial source of scores of social services in the fields of education, health care, housing, labor market, care of the aged, sport and leisure, and so forth. In fact, the notion of welfare has been broadened steadily after World War II, which gave the concept "welfare state" an almost oceanic meaning. As a British observer remarked, "it covers almost everyone in need, from unmarried mothers to deprived children, from old persons unable to look after themselves to deserted wives with dependent children, from ex-prisoners unable to obtain work to physically or mentally handicapped adults, from, homeless immigrants to problem families."[7]

In sum, it is very difficult to give a precise and formal definition of the welfare state in advance. However, it is possible and sensible to list its main dimensions and components briefly, if only to avoid an unmanageably broad discussion. Thus, in this book the concept of welfare state refers to these characteristics:

- the welfare state is more than just state or government, but refers beyond the administrative realm also to the economic, the social, and even the cultural realms of modern life;
- economically, the welfare state is a mixed system, i.e., one based upon a relatively free market in which private businesses operate, yet regulated statutorily and at times financially subsidized by a central government;
- socially, citizens are entitled to collective social services, which the state guarantees statutorily and which, where necessary, it finances through taxes and excises on the basis of social solidarity; welfare services can be and often are extended by nongovernmental, private organizations, but these remain dependent on state subsidies and subjected to statutory rules and controls;
- culturally, the welfare state is more than a system of distributive justice for the sake of equality, it is the result of the moral attempt to establish a civilized society in which, to use the words of Lord Beveridge, people are insured against the four scourges of humanity, "Want, Disease, Ignorance, Squalor and Idleness."[8]

Two Basic Types

Various typologies of different welfare states have been constructed. It is particularly difficult to cluster nations into different types of welfare state. Richard Titmuss did not fuss too much over this, and maybe he was the wiser for it. In any case, he simply distinguished two broad categories, which I found quite useful: (1) *residual welfare states*, which take responsibility for general welfare in a targeted manner, only when the family and/or the market fail to function properly, consequently limiting its scope of operation to marginal and deserving social groups or categories; and (2) *institutional welfare states* which is universalistic, assumes responsibility for a broad spectrum of social services, and takes up a highly organized and deeply institutionalized role in the distribution of these services to which in principle all citizens are entitled. The residual welfare state is characteristic of most American states, the institutional welfare state can be found in most Western European countries, that is in Northern Europe and up until the 1980s. Naturally, the institutional welfare state knows countless varieties, depending on what is being emphasized and put in the center. Scores of national differences can therefore be enumerated, but it is questionable if that is very helpful. In any case, this book focuses on the institutional welfare state in Northwestern Europe, although I prefer the concept of *comprehensive*, or *intensive and extensive* welfare state, because the adjective *institutional* is misleading. After all, Titmuss's residual welfare state must also be organized lest it fragment and fade away. Other typifications—according to three dominant political ideologies (Esping-Anderson) and according to geographical regions (Leibfried) will be discussed later.

The Basic Rationale

The successive chapters of this book can be read independently, but they are formulated according to a basic rationale. Apart from the leading idea of a Democratic Triangle, the balance of which had been disturbed by the comprehensive welfare state of the 1960s and 1970s, the main focus is on the cultural and moral dimensions of the welfare state. Chapter 1 argues that its historical roots go back as far as the sixteenth century. The evolution of care is described as an ongoing rationalization but the development has not been a unilinear one. In the progressive rationalization there are scores of regressive tendencies which in fact demonstrates the basic ambiguity of the welfare state. This point will be further elaborated in chapter 2.

The moral factor is discussed next in chapter 3. Three analytic, nonempirical (*ideal*) types of ethos are confronted with the comprehensive welfare state and the presence or absence of an elective affinity is established. There is, it is being concluded, a strong elective affinity between an immoralist type of ethos and the comprehensive welfare state. The waning of the intensive and extensive welfare state, and the reinvigoration of civil society, it is argued, might strengthen again the moralist type of ethos. If in terms of the Democratic Triangle the market would be reinvigorated at the expense of both the state and civil society, it might be expected that the amoralist ethos type would gain predominance.

After roughly 1980 the comprehensive welfare state of most Western European societies came under fire. Internal and external forces made a fundamental transformation unavoidable. Chapter 4 discusses the main processes that have led to this waning of the comprehensive welfare state.

Usually the comprehensive welfare state is criticized in mainly economic-financial and political-administrative terms: it allegedly generated a cumbersome, highly centralized bureaucracy and an unmanageable public spending, much to the detriment of the market and civil society. These arguments are well known by now and will not be repeated. Chapter 5 instead follows in line with the general argument of the book the cultural and moral transformations of the comprehensive welfare state. There is the pressing need to transcend the simple, liberal dictum "less state, more market." We are beyond the comprehensive welfare state and in need of a balanced Democratic Triangle in which the constitutional state occupies its proper position vis-à-vis both the market and civil society. Democracy itself is at stake if but one of its three corners is weakened, as was the case prior to 1980 when the state occupied an overbearing position in the triangle, and again in the 1980s and early 1990s, when the market was the leading factor in society.

Notes

1. Cf. the much quoted essay by Michel Albert, *Capitalism against Capitalism*, translated by P. Haviland (London: Whurr Publishers [1991]1993). It juxtaposes the economic "Rhine model" and the economic "American model" which allegedly are two basically different specimens of capitalism with different time perspectives (long-run versus short-run) and different welfare provisions (compre-

hensive versus limited). It stands in a postwar, French-intellectual tradition which was always fond of contrasting European and American culture. In this contrast Europe is always adjudicated the socioeconomically, politically, and morally favorable position.

2. G. Esping-Andersen, *The Three Worlds of Welfare Capitalism*, (Princeton, NJ: Princeton University Press, 1990), p. 45.

3. *Ibid.,* p. 107.

4. *Ibid.,* p. 59.

5. *Ibid.*, p. 60.

6. Substantial rationality comes very close to the German *Verstehen*, the meaning-ful understanding of reality. Since such understanding is only possible with the help of values which structure reality in terms of "good" and "evil," "beautiful" and "ugly," "true" and "false," "civilized" and "brutal," and so forth. Weber called substantial rationality *Wertrationalität*, or value-rationality.

7. William A. Robson, *Welfare State and Welfare Society: Illusion and Reality* (London: George Allen and Unwin, 1976), p. 31.

8. Cf. William H. Beveridge, *Voluntary Action. A Report on Methods of Social Advance* (New York: Macmillan Co., 1948), p. 6.

1

The Rationalization of Care

The Welfare State as Historical Phenomenon

Caring for fellow human beings is apparently a "natural" thing to do, originating in the fundamental fact that the newly born are in need of parental care for a relatively long period of time. Reversedly, up until the birth of industrial society the aged were in need of care by their children, or by default of offspring by the charity of consociates. This again demonstrates the basic fact that care is never exclusively altruistic but caught in exchange relationships.

If care is never exclusively altruistic, it is also rarely an exclusively private matter. The education of the young, the care for the sick and the indigent, for instance, have in the past been seen also as a collective responsibility. It is often believed that care guaranteed and financed by the state originates in the industrial society, but this is quite wrong. As the Elizabethan Poor Law illustrates, there has been a remarkably early concurrence of private charity and public care in the history of Europe ever since the age of feudalism. It was, in a sense, a case of collective rational choice. Even feudalism is in the history of care a remarkable phenomenon, since the bond of mutual assistance between lord and vassal was based upon distinct shared interests. Moreover, as we shall see instantly, this bond of mutual dependence and assistance demonstrated through its contractual nature an early form of rationality.

Particularly if one wants to grasp the cultural and moral dimensions of the welfare state undergirding its economic and political framework, one should take the history of private and public care in Europe into account. As I shall argue presently, this history has predominantly been a process of progressive rationalization. However, this chapter intends to discuss the rationalization of care in some broadly sketched contours only. It does not pretend to be historically complete, but tries to highlight the main stages of the development of care from the days of the feudal contract between lord and vassal until the twentieth century. Hopefully, this historical sketch will illustrate the fact that the Western welfare state is the product of a relatively long process of European development.

Usually historical accounts of the welfare state start with Bismarck at the end of the nineteenth centtury, who, alhough a staunch conservative, initiated social legislation in order to pacify social unrest among the workers and to bypass organized labor. Or Lloyd George's liberal social insurances legislation at the beginning of the twentieth century is taken as the actual start of the European welfare state. Others again view the end of World War II as the actual start of the welfare state. This chapter places the development of state-provided care in a much broader perspective.

Two Types of Care

In this chapter the historical data pertain almost exclusively to the Anglo-Saxon world. There is a valid reason for this. Although the individual European welfare states developed their own patterns within the rationalization of care from charity to the welfare state, we can observe a common pattern which in fact is demonstrated most clearly by the British case. Here the Elizabethan Poor Law set the tone for the pre-industrial arrangements of state-provided care, and here the Industrial Revolution began which, as is well known, accelerated the process of rationalization, not in the least the rationalization of care. Moreover, the British welfare state, and the Keynesean economics that bore it, stood model for most postwar, comprehensive welfare states in the rest of Western Europe. It thus makes sense to focus on Great Britain, when the development of care from medieval charity to contemporary statutory services is surveyed.

It has been argued that during the Middle Ages and in early modernity urban governments began to develop programs of material aid, social security, and hygienic care for reasons of calculated interest. The socioeconomic and cultural elites feared the social unrest of the poor masses, and tried to alleviate it by various social programs, much like Bismarck who in the nineteenth century initiated the *Sozialstaat* in order to pacify the rising working class in industrializing Germany.[1]

This interpretation, as we will see, is not wrong but somewhat one-sided and limited. Behind or beneath it lurks the rather traditionally marxist and metaphysical notion of an unavoidable class-dominated conflict of interests between the powerful "haves" and the powerless "have nots." These rational choice motives did indeed recur constantly during the long history of England's Poor Law. It can, of course, not be denied that arrangements of statutory care were set up in order to minimalize the chances of social unrest. Bismarck too did indeed lay the foundations of the German welfare state in order to curb the power of the working class. We, however, should not dismiss the genuinely religious and humanitarian motives that throughout the history of Western Europe have inspired people to engage in actions of care and charity. They were in fact at work before urban patricians began to worry about the possible social unrest among the artisans and workers within the walls of their cities. Charity continued to work in modernity as a strong moral force, as is exemplified, for example, in the teachings of the Fabians, various bodies of Christian Social Democracy, and, in particular, the Anglo-Saxon voluntary associations devoted to community service, such as the Red Cross and the Salvation Army. In any case charity is viewed and interpreted in this chapter as an autonomous, moral force that preluded the welfare state of the twentieth century which, incidentally, in its turn contributed much to its corrosion.[2]

Throughout the ages, care has been seen in the European orbit as both a favor and a right. In the Middle Ages, for instance, much attention was given to the care of the destitute and indigent— the poor, the sick, widows, and orphans—because they were seen as religious symbols, as representatives of the people loved and favored by Jesus Christ. The poor and indigent possessed a metaphysical surplus value, and thus care was viewed primarily as part of a religiously motivated and experienced charity. The destitute and indigent were religiously and morally, not legally though, entitled to this kind of care. This is difficult to understand for fully modernized people. Today, care within the context of the welfare state has become a nonreligious and amoral right—a social right. In fact, charity has become morally suspicious. It is associated with patronizing beneficence, and criticized for fighting the symptoms not the causes of socioeconomic arrearage.

It is against this background that we can construct two ideal-types: *care-as-favor* (charity based upon religious or humanitarian morality) administered to needy individuals and *care-as-right* (social security statutorily founded upon law and the state) administered to statistically determinable categories which are defined as cases. We shall see next that the rationalization of care constitutes a process of development which takes place, as it were, on a continuum between these two opposite poles: from care-as-favor at the one end to care-as-right at the other. This is a constructed continuum, the poles of which are analytic and heuristic, not empirical. Care-as-favor is in the setting of a modern welfare state not absent, just as the dimension of care-as-right was not absent in the days of traditional care and charity.

As to care-as-right, it was indeed present in the Middle Ages, since the feudal system was based upon a semi-legal contract between liege lord and vassal. As Bloch illustrated convincingly in his seminal study of feudal society, the relationship between lord and vassal was initially a contractual and rational one, to the mutual advantage of the two contract partners.[3] The self-interests of both were served by it. In this contract the liege lord's care of the vassal and his family in times of adversity and hardship was ascertained as guarantee and security. In return, the vassal would serve his lord by participating in war raids, by repairing the roads in and surrounding the manor, and by other services. Bloch argues that the feudal system soon grew complex and vague to the detriment of its legal dimensions and safeguards. Rational law was pushed to the background and evaporated eventually together with the dimension of care-as-right.

Likewise, care-as-favor (charity) is not totally absent in our modern, industrialized society. A prime example of this is, of course, the Salvation Army in which the material care and succor to the homeless and destitute in the big cities has always been seen as a means to arrive eventually at the immaterial salvation of the soul:

> Conceptions of charity can even in this day and age be very traditional, and yet receive worldwide recognition and esteem. After she received the Nobel Peace Price in 1979, the Albanian-born Mother Theresa of Calcutta said in a televised interview that we ought to be grateful for the many poor and destitute in this world, because they symbolize Christ's poverty and function as the meaningful aim of our Christian neighborly love. For someone living in a welfare state in which work, minimal income, sufficient health care, decent housing, good education and a decent standard of living for the seniors of society are the taken-for-granted components of a civilized society, these words are totally ununderstandable. They seem to belong to a different world—a world shared, incidentally, by another Nobel laureate who sacrificed fame and wealth as a musician, physician and church minister in Europe and worked as a physician in a little African village: Albert Schweitzer of Lambarene. His rather traditional conception of care was also deemed worthy of receiving worldwide attention and appraisal. He received the Nobel Peace Prize in 1952.

This traditional type of care-as-favor is still present, albeit it in a less religious setting, as in service clubs like Rotary, Kiwanis, Lions, Zonta, and Soroptimists. These are voluntary, nongovernmental associations which focus on the well-being and welfare of the immediate surrounding community. Their morally inspired service to the community consists in many instances of charitable activities.[4]

In traditional, preindustrial times care-as-favor was executed predominantly by religiously inspired volunteers and amateurs, not rarely women from the higher echelons of society who, for whatever reason, had remained single and could not participate in the production process precisely because they belonged to the higher societal stratum. They often engaged in acts of charity driven by religious motivations. The Beguines in the Netherlands are a telling example. They were a semi-religious order that offered a home and social shelter to widows and unmarried women unfit for the labor market of those days but very fit for the care of the poor and the sick in their community:

> The word "beguine" (in Dutch *begijn*) derives in all probability from the old-French *bège*, which means "gray," or "light brown." This refers to the color of the simple gown the beguines wore. Their movement began in the twelfth century in the emerging Dutch cities, in particular in the South, the present territory of Belgium. Due to the crusades and the incessant warfare in Europe in which in particular the nobility of these parts of Europe was involved—the so-called *Brabanciones*—many young women were widow or single. There was, at the same time, a strong leaning towards mysticism and a yearning for a fundamental reformation of the organized Roman Catholic church. Rather than marrying below their class, these upper-class women combined their mystic propensity with a semi-monastic style of life, while serving the poor and the sick. The first beguine communities were attached to male monasteries in the cities, but soon they were driven to organize themselves in so-called *beguinages* (in Dutch, *begijnenhofjes*), often located next to or in the vicinity of a church or a hospital. The movement spread out over Europe, in particular in Germany where, however, strong heretical (manicheistic) influences intruded and gained dominance. In fact, the beguines had to be defended in Rome against suspicions of being a disguised heretical movement. The Council of Vienne (1311) condemned them, but the Curia in Rome soon realized that the Dutch beguines were a genuinely orthodox community. Pope John XXII protected them with a special papal bull in 1318.
>
> There were also male counterparts of the beguins: the *beghards*, or *boghards* who also lived in semi-monastic communities in the cities. There were beghards working in hospitals, but many were also active in crafts, in particular in the production of cloth.
>
> The beguines and beghards vanished as semi-monastic orders during the French Revolution. Today, only their beguinages, like the ones in Amsterdam and Breda, have survived modernization as architectural oases of tranquillity in the middle of modern urban life.[5]

Charity was also taken up by lay brothers and sisters who did not adhere to a semi-monastic style of life but were organized in various orders of knighthood, such as the Order of the Knights of St. John and the German Order. They emerged after the crusades and their members set themselves the task to tend to the sick and the poor.[6]

Next to voluntarism, moralism was a predominant feature of this kind of care. The spender of charity, it was believed, underwent a moral purification, whereas its recipients were supposed to express their gratitude. This ties up with a third characteristic. Between the provider and the recipient of this kind of care there was a personal bond based upon inequality and often patronizing paternalism. In fact, it was often believed that illness and poverty were caused by sin and moral weakness. The fourth characteristic of this kind of charity is the upshot of that fateful belief: recipients were held personally responsible for their plight and thereby made dependent upon the providers of succor, unable, of course, to claim such care, let alone to express misgivings and critique. Keep in mind that there were no formal and general criteria with regard to the categories of people who were and were not entitled to care and succor. The dispense thereof was focused upon individuals and remained rather contingent.

All this stands in sharp contrast to the dominant features of the opposite type of care. Care-as-right is not based upon a religious sense of calling and responsibility on the part of volunteers and amateurs. Rationally trained professionals dispense this care, and in order to be entitled to it, the recipients have to fit preestablished, formal and bureaucratic categories and criteria. Moral sentiments are absent. If there is still a trace of morality left in the care of a modern welfare state, in which this type of care is, of course, very dominant, it has been generalized to such an extent as to being well-nigh unrecognizable. Concepts like "justice," "equality," and "solidarity" are often employed to refer to the legitimizing moral foundations of the welfare state. They are generally seen these days as liberal, if not left-of-center values. It could be argued also that their origins are religious and even biblical. Yet, in a comprehensive welfare state it is exceedingly hard for the common citizen to experience these basic values as concrete legitimations of the system. If one examines one's own heavily taxed paycheck with its numerous additional deductions through which the welfare state is financed, it takes quite an imagination to view and accept them as one's personal, concrete contribution to the values of justice, equality, and solidarity.

The modern providers of care are predominantly professionals who deliver and distribute their services to "clients" and "customers" on a sort of "welfare market." After a relatively long period of professional training in which they acquire the necessary diplomas, these quartenary-service professionals obtain state-guaranteed licenses. They are the "producers" and "distributors" of professional care to which preestablished, bureaucratically determined categories of "care consumers" are entitled. The state—the welfare state—controls, legalizes and above all finances all this scrupulously. The important point here is that the social rights invested in the welfare state are not just beneficial to the recipient citizens of the welfare state, but serve also and in many cases even primarily the interests of the experts and professionals of care and succor. They occupy crucial and often powerful positions in the ever-expanding, nonproductive, quaternary sector of modern society. They are the vanguard of what has come to be called the New Class, or because of their usually thorough schooling, the Knowledge Class.[7] We will return to this point later.

The moral dimension is important here. The more the package of care expands, the more the producers and consumers of it will be inclined to push their own private interests to the foreground, often to the detriment of the responsibility one bears as citizen towards the common and public interests of society as a whole. Understandably, the brunt of responsibility as to the quality and quantity of the services is pushed aside by both, preferably in the direction of the state. In a highly developed, comprehensive welfare state welfare is, in the end, an affair of the state.

Whereas care-as-favor is characterized by personal dependence and personal inequality, it is typical of care-as-right to be characterized by formal, bureaucratic dependence and by formal inequality. If he is in need of care and succor, the citizen of a welfare state depends on various specialized organizations and its bureaucracies, and in particular, of course, on their professional experts and specialists. Just by their highly specialized and esoteric knowledge and techniques, these professionals have a disproportionate advantage over their clients. It has been argued that this kind of professionalism contributed to the disabling of people.[8]

After we have thus discussed the two opposite poles of the continuum, we must now fill in the space between them. For clarity's sake I shall distinguish four stages: (1) *charity*, typical of a medieval, feudal society; (2) *self-help*, typical of the Reformation first, and then of the Enlightenment; (3) *social insurance*, typical of Liberalism from the eighteenth century until approximately 1950; and (4) *social security*, typical of the welfare state after 1950 until roughly 1980. It bears repeating that the next sections do not pretend to be historically complete or exact. The distinguished four stages are ideal-typical constructions for the sake of understanding the rationalization of care.

Charity

In a sense, the political and socioeconomic system of feudalism can be seen as a remedy against the progressive disintegration of the Carolingian empire after the death of Charles the Great.[9] The system was based upon the previously mentioned contractual relationship of feudal lord and vassal: in exchange for protection, care, and often a piece of land, a vassal offered his services to a feudal lord. It was a remarkably rational, contractual system based upon mutual interests. Initially this was a personal and non-hereditary arrangement consisting of mutual rights and duties. As it occurred in a great and complex multiplicity, the vassal in one relationship often being the lord again in another (subinfeudation), these exchange relationships gradually led to some sort of socioeconomic and legal order. By hindsight these fragmented networks of feudal bonds look almost "postmodern."

Barraclough argued convincingly that Charles the Great left after his death a vast empire that lacked any trace of organization and infrastructure. Looked at from a modern public policy perspective, the Carolingian empire was indeed wrought with anarchistic chaos. Between the ninth and eleventh centuries this very weak megastructure which covered almost all of today's Europe, came under recurrent attacks from all sides: Saracens from the south, Magyars from the east and Vikings from the north. Very soon the skilled seafaring Vikings in particular marauded almost all coasts of Europe, including even some Mediterranean shores. The empire Charles had left was unable to repel these attacks successfully. The Europeans in their hamlets, towns, and cities were defenseless and on their own. The feudal system of lord-vassal relationships filled up the void. It provided the continent with a minimum of order and defensibility, albeit in an extremely fragmented and thus vulnerable way.

This system, it should be noted, was not a familial one. In some respects it even stood at right angles to the family. In the early Middle Ages family ties were still solid and influential. But, as Bloch argues, families were not organized as unilinear clans or *gentes*, but consisted instead of relationships of both the wife and the husband. As a social system they, therefore, lacked coherence, strength, and defensibility.

The mutual bonds remained rather emotional and could easily disintegrate due to feuds and similar familial conflicts. The feudal system, on the contrary, not being based on irrational blood ties but on rational, contractual relationships, managed initially to function as an integrating force. They did contribute to the much needed defensibility.[10] However, over time the system deteriorated and finally collapsed due to the disintegrating process of subinfeudation—vassals becoming lords to lower vassals becoming lords to again lower vassals, et cetera. It led in the *Ancien Régime* to the pulverization of society and facilitated the emergence of absolutism.

Within the lord-vassal relationship care, as we saw, evolved initially as a remarkably rational type of legal responsibility on the part of the lord. The feudal lord was obliged to guarantee the safety and welfare of his vassals and their families. In a sense, his estate—the *seigneurie*, the *manor*— functioned as a mini-welfare "state." Yet, one should hasten to add, this kind of rational care began to fade away while the Middle Ages progressed in time. The dependence, coercion, and exploitation of the farmers in particular became very typical of the feudal system, to which the recurrent peasant revolts testified. Even though the author clearly takes side with the feudal establishment, the *Chronicles* of Jean Froissart (1337–1410) give a lively picture of the frustrations of the farmers of his days.[11] Soon the same fate befell the early proletariat in the emerging cities.

Meanwhile, what happened to the countless individuals who were not part of a lord-vassal relationship, who could not fall back upon the protection and succor of family members, and who did not belong to one or the other religious order? These were the widows and orphans, the errand laborers and seasonal workers, the monks who had deserted or were dismissed from their monastery, and the students who had dropped out of the university, as well as the class- and estateless riffraff of medieval society—the lepers, insane, and mendicants. Many of them belonged to a category of people called by one historian *les misérables dans l'occident médiéval*.[12] They formed a chaotic mass of indigents who were dependent almost exclusively on charity. This charity was, of course, a nonrational, if not irrational, highly moralistic and religiously motivated care-as-favor. Incidentally, the numbers of these charity-dependent *misérables* were unstable and unpredictable, since they depended on the success or failure of the economy. Since medieval people were not able to understand, let alone control economic processes and business cycles, there were recurrent waves of inflation and malaise which then immediately augmented the numbers of *misérables*. At times their numbers could assume enormous proportions. The greatest misfortunes of those days were (physical and mental) illness and poverty. They consequently functioned as the prime targets of religiously motivated charities. The sick who until the sixteenth century were merely nursed, not treated therapeutically, were held morally responsible for their disease. There was a general conviction that illness was caused by the fact that one had consciously or unconsciously succumbed to the seductions of the devil. Before a patient was placed in a hospital bed, he had to go to confession and communion.[13] The hospital building itself resembled a church architecturally. In France it bore and still bears the name "Hôtel Dieu." Entering the hospital as a patient involved a rather radical separation from the rest of society, particularly of course in the case of contagious diseases. Contagious patients were set apart in special asylums like the leper colonies. Entrance to such an institution was often coupled with a kind of funeral service. It has been reported that a leprous patient was laid down in a coffin placed on a bier in the chapel. Entering the colony meant that one was to all intents and purposes socially dead. Against this background, the importance of the previously mentioned beguines, who often lived next to leper colonies and took care of the patients there, can hardly be underrated.

Hospitals in the Middle Ages lacked any trace of structural differentiation or specialization. In fact, the institution functioned mainly as a reception center, indeed a *hôtel Dieu*, for scores of societal border cases—poor patients, vagabonds, beggars, homeless orphans, poor pilgrims, mentally disturbed people, seasonal drunkards, and so on. Gradually, however, differentiation set in. The hospital became the place for the poor sick and the indigent elderly, while the other categories were taken care of in orphanages, workhouses, and city jails. This process of differentiation was not concluded until the nineteenth century.

The notion of charity is, of course, immediately associated with private initiatives, and in a medieval and early-modern context one is inclined to conclude that charity is primarily, if not exclusively an affair of religiously motivated individuals and private organizations. This was indeed the case for most of medieval and early modern Europe, with the exception of England where in the seventeenth century charity became a state-initiated activity. The story of the British *Poor Law* is well known. Due to the ecclesiatic secession from Rome, eventually realized by Henry VIII, a national church headed by the monarch was set up. The ensuing unity of church and state gave religious charity a remarkable etatist dimension, which for Europe in those days was unique, since charity had been in general a private, religious, largely unorganized and often quite chaotic affair.

During the reign of Henry VIII attempts had already been made to arrive at a state legislation for the relief of the poor and indigent. This was then realized under his daughter's reign by the "Acte for the Reliefe of the Poore" of 1601. In the ensuing centuries this so-called *Poor Law* was revised recurrently, but its basic pattern remained intact until 1948. In that year the "National Assistance Act" ushered in the British post-war Welfare State.

The Poor Law presented not only a remarkable legalization of reli-giously motivated private charity, but was also the result of sociopolitical motives. Through this law which apparently was just one item in a much broader economic program,[14] the ruling elites hoped to curb so-cial unrest, particularly in the countryside. It served, Marshall argued, to preserve rather than to change the existing social and economic or-der. Moreover, since its execution and administration were decentral-ized and laid in the hands of the local elites who functioned as "the overseers of the poor," the Poor Law served the self-interests of the possessing classes who saw themselves as the "natural rulers" of the country, first and foremost. Incidentally, to some social historians this is the basic pattern, if not the hidden agenda, of all social security ar-rangements issued by national states.[15] As was said before, this point of view is not incorrect but a bit one-sided. The social historian Bruce arrived at a more balanced conclusion, when he discussed the Poor Law: "It was in fact a combination of compassion and fear of distur-bance that brought about the Elizabethan poor law system, a combina-tion of social amelioration and police deterrence that might be said to be the ultimate basis of the Welfare State."[16]

An important component of the Poor Law was the provision of work by means of various facilities for home industry, and through work-houses as well which were initially not the infamous institutions into which they developed in later days. In fact, employment became such a crucial issue in public policy that the relief of the poor and indigent was referred back to private, religious charity again. Christopher Hill at any rate drew from this development the following balanced conclu-sion: "In the Middle Ages relief of the poor had been a matter for chari-ty, dispensed through the Church. The State which took over so many of the Church's functions at the Reformation, was reluctant to assume this one. The Poor Law was a minimum framework aimed at providing sufficient employment to prevent disorder; but relief of poverty was left mainly to private initiative."[17]

Gradually a distinction emerged between two categories of people deserving care. Disabled persons, children, and widows were labeled as *impotent poor*, whereas physically and mentally healthy adults able to work but unemployed were called *able-bodied poor*. The former category remained dependent on private and religiously motivated charity, while the latter were subjected summarily to the Poor Law of the state and its increasingly harsh conditions. The test for the able-bodied poor was exclusively physical and mental. The notion of a structurally conditioned unemployment did not arise. Unemployment was in those days not a socioeconomic and structural but a moral phenomenon. Those who were judged to be able-bodied and mentally fit, were summarily sent to the workhouse, where they were subjected to the at times very stern regime of the Poor Law. Soon the workhouses resembled and were often indeed envisaged as houses of criminal correction.

Self-Help

There is no need to review once more the work ethic of Puritanism based upon an "inner-worldly asceticism" (Max Weber). It is equally superfluous to emphasize its rational nature, its focus on the individual, and its contribution to the modernization (rationalization) of the Western world. However, in the context of the present discussion we must underline the strong emphasis of Puritanism upon the moral responsibility of the individual: man is to be held personally accountable for his deeds and words, and is supposed to maintain his private existence and the existence of those dependent upon him, the members of his family in the first place but the employees in his shop or place of business as well. The dictum typical of Puritanism was: "Help yourself, so help you God." The Puritan does not work industriously in order to gain a place in heaven, he is not active in good deeds of charity in order to secure his salvation after death. Original sin could not be wiped out by such earthly endeavors. As a result, there was a strong sense of Destiny and Fate in the Puritanic view of the world. As to salvation, Puritans had nothing else to do than to hope and trust that God would have predestined them for heaven. Hard labor and good deeds served exclusively the honor of God with whom Puritans were connected individually and directly, without any intermediaries, such as absolving

priests, saints, rituals and sacraments. This, of course, is a very individualistic and rational view of man. Weber argued, as is well known, that
this peculiar ethic with its emphasis upon labor, inner-worldly asceticism and rational calculation stood in a strong, yet unintended elective
affinity to the spirit of capitalism, and thereby contributed to the rise of
high capitalism in the Western world.

In this type of ethic there is, of course, little room for compassionate
charity. On the contrary, poverty was viewed increasingly as the result
of moral weakness: everyone who is able and willing to work hard, will
not suffer from want and poverty. If someone is indigent and poor, his
misery is due to moral weakness. Unless indigence and misery befall
one undeservedly, as in the case of a severe illness, a tragic accident, or
the death of a family breadwinner, one has apparently not learned (or
has been unwilling) to work industriously. If a person is physically or
mentally disabled, or otherwise helpless without personal guilt (widows and orphans, for instance), he or she is entitled to compassion and
charity dispensed by the church.

This chain of thought was taken over by the Enlightenment in a secularized version, and continued to exert its influence deeply into the twentieth century, propagated as it was by classical liberalism. God and
predestination were pushed aside by the Autonomous Individual and the
Invisible Hand. Religious eschatology was likewise succeeded by the
rationalist notion of Progress. The latter, in particular, had grave consequences for the poor and indigent. There was, Bruce wrote, an "increasing impatience with the poor as feckless obstacles to the steady progress
of economic improvement."[18] The inherent individualism deserves attention, as it is unable or not prepared to take into account the structural and
conjunctural, and thus non-individual and amoral causes of poverty.[19] It
was not before the end of the nineteenth century that one began to search
for causes behind the symptoms. Up till then one preached often in a
secularized vein "the gospel of self-help" (Richard Niebuhr),[20] an ideology, incidentally, that survived the nineteenth century and continued to
influence bourgeois thought and practice well into the twentieth century.

Like the Poor Law this rationalistic and individualistic ethic divided
the indigent into two broad categories: the "undeserving poor" who are
in need of help and succor (the physically and mentally impaired, the
widows and orphans foremost), and "people who would not work",
often labeled as "lazy rogues." The second category is, it was believed,
to be put to work, if necessary by force and coercion. The workhouses
of the Poor Law got a new lease on life.

Yet, one should not misunderstand Puritanic individualism. It was not the intention of the doctrine of self-help to have people withdraw from society at large, serving exclusively their individual and private interests. On the contrary, it was believed that the Puritanic individual should contribute to the common wealth and welfare and heed the common interest rather than the self-interest.[21] In a sermon held in the House of Commons in 1643, it was said that every citizen had the duty "to contribute his abilities of what kind soever to be serviceable to the community."[22] Puritans did in fact organize themselves and begin to exert a distinct influence on society. Dissenting Puritans formed scores of associations which aimed not only at the defense of their own particular interests but also at the improvement and salvation of society in general. In their initial period—the sixteenth and seventeenth centuries—these associations were more sect-like than church-like, and thus had a strong voluntaristic bent. As is well known, these Puritanic voluntary associations with their individualistic and moralistic ethic strongly influenced American society—an influence which is still discernible today and which, as we shall see later, precluded the emergence of a comprehensive welfare state.

This is not the place for a detailed discussion of the attitude of the Puritans towards the care of the poor and indigent. I limit myself to a few exemplary comments. The spirit of the Poor Law which distinguished the "impotent poor" from the "lazy rogues" remained intact and was even acerbated. But when Puritanism came to political power under Cromwell, it came into conflict with the propertied gentry that administered the poor relief under the regiment of the Poor Law. Their power in the provinces was taken over by the Major Generals who then were responsible for the relief of the poor.[23] However, we may assume safely that this change of power did not really change the plight of the poor and unemployed. On the contrary, these predominantly lower-middle class Puritans generally lacked the more liberal attitudes of the propertied gentry and rather tightened the screws of control and punishment.

The Puritanic notion of self-help underwent a decisive transformation during the rise of utilitarianism as professed by classical liberalism in the nineteenth century. One began to believe—and a belief it certainly was—that the good of the community, thus the general interest, would be served best, if individuals would focus rationally on the fullest possible realization of their private happiness. This was the idea of a well-understood self-interest. It was furthermore believed that there was a natural harmony between individual self-interest and collective, societal interest, that self-interest well understood would be in natural harmony with collective interest. The economic reality of the market had been discovered, and it was believed that the market was driven and kept alive through its own laws, just as nature was. The metaphor of the Invisible Hand, an obvious descendant of the predestining God of the Puritans, was coined in order to introduce a secular force which could and would establish a natural harmony between private and collective interests.

Incidentally, one ought to heed the notion of *laissez-faire* which at this point is usually introduced into the discussion.[24] Jeremy Bentham, often branded as the ideologue of *laissez-faire*, believed that labor was the main source of affluence and happiness. Therefore, social policy ought to be geared primarily to the safeguarding of this prime economic factor. The principle of the greatest good for the largest amount of people could, in his view, not be left exclusively to private initiatives. In fact, it had to be made operable in close co-operation with the state. This meant, contrary to the idea of state *laissez-faire*, that the indigent who were physically or mentally ill ought to receive state supplied assistance with the ultimate purpose of regaining strength and health. He even proposed to install a State Ministry for Indigence Relief![25] This social ministry was, in all likelihood, a policy counterpart of his notorious Panopticon which was meant to be the perfect penitentiary.[26] In any case, the state in Bentham's view was not at all a passive factor.

Meanwhile, during the second half of the eighteenth and first half of the nineteenth century the efficacy of the Poor Law came under ever louder criticism. Because its execution was strongly decentralized and poorly professionalized, abuse of its provisions, critics claimed, mounted. The critique sounds quite familiar: public finances were put under too much pressure due to the allegedly too generously distributed assistance, while the poor were marginalized and demoralized as they lost their independence progressively and resorted to general passivity. It is called nowadays "welfare dependence." However, it was argued also that the poor and unemployed were unable to support themselves and their dependents, becoming progressively entangled in a fatal, downward spiral from which they could not escape within the context of the Poor Law.

Put under pressure by this critique the British government installed in 1832 a committee that had to formulate proposals for a drastic reform of the Poor Law. One of the main proposals of the committee was a by then rather familiar one: state-provided assistance was to be distributed only among the "impotent poor," and had to be refused to the "able bodied" who were physically and mentally fit, yet dependent upon succor and assistance. The committee came forward with various policy measures, two of which became the cornerstones of a new Poor Law, ratified in 1834: first, the amount of assistance ought to be lower than the lowest wages so that the relief would remain pure necessity; second, workhouses were to be set up in which the "able bodied" unemployed who had received relief before were set to work coercively.[27] The Elizabethan institutions of forced labor, the workhouses, were now transformed openly into "houses of correction."

These measures were intended to act primarily as deterrents. People had to be made aware of the fact that they better helped themselves before the state would step in under the aegis of the reformed Poor Law. Again, the awareness of structural and conjunctural causes of unemployment remained still absent, mainly due to a lack of proper economic knowledge and a moralistic view of the world. The unemployed were seen and treated as antisocial elements in need of correction: "Families were to be separated, workhouse clothes worn, silence preserved at meals, all visiting or visitors prohibited and smoking and beer drinking not allowed. Adequate food and shelter were to be provided, but that was all, and adequacy was not to be interpreted liberally."[28] Marshall, who viewed social history in terms of the evolution of citizenship, emphasized the sociopolitical dimension of the new Poor Law: claimants of assistance actually forfeited their citizenship. "The Poor Law treated the claims of the poor, not as an integral part of the rights of the citizen, but as an alternative to them—as claims which could be met only if the claimants ceased to be citizens in any sense of the word. For paupers forfeited in practice the civil right of personal liberty, by internment in the workhouse, and they forfeited by law any political rights they might possess.... Those who accepted relief must cross the road that separated the community of citizens from the outcast company of the destitute."[29] The emphasis in all this was, as Beveridge phrased it lucidly, on the poor, not on poverty.[30] The poor were, to all intents and purposes, treated as illegal aliens and outcasts.

The 1834 revision of the Poor Law had interesting consequences. To begin with, those individuals who despite hard work slipped back into poverty, but tried to stay out of the workhouse, remained dependent on charity. Due to the retreat of the state which, of course, was part of the Poor Law reformation of 1834, charitative private initiatives prospered more than ever before. The increase of these initiatives was such that it necessitated in due time some measure of organized coordination. In 1869 the "Charity Organization Society" was developed.[31] Moreover, in order to stay out of the dreaded workhouse, workers intensified their pursuit of antiquated measures to insure themselves and their dependents collectively against economic and social calamities, such as illness, disablement, unemployment and death. In other words, there occurred a certain privatization of social insurance. It was an organized self-help that eventually led to formation of large funds of mutual aid which were not public but private securities. Looking at the present situation after the comprehensive welfare state from this historical perspective, one cannot but feel a sense of history repeating itself.

Social Insurance

In Great Britain these collective insurances emerged within the framework of the *Friendly Societies* which were mutual aid associations with rather ancient roots. The history of these societies is remarkable, and goes back to the seventeenth century, when they served mainly two goals: conviviality and the assurance of a decent funeral. To this end regular payments were deposited in a communal fund, not rarely administered by the owner of the local pub. After 1834 these Friendly Societies developed into often nationwide organizations which offered socioeconomic insurance in the case of illness, disablement, old-age, and death. Insurance against unemployment incidentally became the prerogative of the trade unions which emerged later. In any case, these associations of mutual aid functioned as links between the individualistic and moralistic self-help of Puritanism and classical liberalism on the one hand, and the twentieth-century welfare state on the other. Thus, they presented a decisive phase on the continuum that runs from care as charitable favor on the one end, to care as a social and citizen right on the other.

Although one of them, the Incorporation of Carters, goes back to 1555, the first Friendly Societies came about in seventeenth-century Calvinist Scotland, whereas in England the first of these societies were set up by Huguenot refugees who, being foreigners, were excluded from the provisions of the Poor Law. "They were driven to self-help," Beveridge explains, and he adds: "In so far as such a motive applied to them it would apply also to Scotland, where public provisions for relief of poverty long lagged behind that of England."[32] As these instances suggest, the Protestant ethic with its emphasis on self-help did come into play, when the Friendly Societies emerged and grew in scope and size.

These associations for collective self-help which until the end of World War II played an important role in Great Britain, particularly in the socioeconomic care of the higher working class and lower middle class, were originally a curious mixture of conviviality and social insurance. Usually organized within one of the crafts, as their names suggest (United General Sea Box, 1634; Fraternity of Dyers, 1670; Goldsmiths's Friendly Society, 1712; Ancient Society of Gardeners, 1716)[33] they adopted the sociable functions and the rituals of the guilds. Yet, they did have a more serious goal as well: the original funeral insurance evolved gradually into a package of various socioeconomic insurances, such as those against illness, disablement, and old-age. Originally, the members' contributions were collected in the places where they used to meet—the inn, the church, and in a rare case even the brothel. In modern times, local chapters merged, and thus gave birth to large, national federations of considerable size. Often these nation-wide funds managed and commanded over substantial assets. As was said before, insurance against unemployment became the prerogative of the trade unions.

In the nineteenth century several of these funds had become so bloated that they were able to pay dividends to their members. Some of them thus developed into saving funds. As early as 1793 the spectacular growth of these associations led to legal regulation: the Act for the Encouragement and Relief of Friendly Societies. It was meant to stimulate but also control these private associations. That remained, as we will see instantly, a favorite preoccupation of the British legislator.

The law of 1793 defined a Friendly Society thus: "A society of good fellowship for the purpose of raising from time to time, by voluntary contributions, a stock or fund for the mutual relief and maintenance of all and every members thereof, in old age, sickeness, and in infirmity, or for the relief of widows and children of deceased members."[34] Beveridge emphasized the fact that the Friendly Societies had a much wider scope than just the assurance of social security: "They have been social clubs; they have been societies concerned with the general welfare of their members; they have been channels for the spirit of voluntary service."[35] Unlike the trade unions, these voluntary associations of mutual assistance were neutral in terms of political ideology and worldview. Beveridge, as we shall see, regretted the fact that these Friendly Societies with their mutual solidarity and common commitment did not play any role in the welfare state that emerged in Great Britain after World War II. He obviously did not realize that this type of voluntarism was gravely at odds with the nature and ethos of the comprehensive welfare state erected after the war.

The attitude of the aristocratic and upper-middle class elites towards the Friendly Societies was quite ambivalent. On the one hand, they supported them as they helped to cut down the financial pressures on the provisions of the Poor Law. This positive evaluation was in fact the main motivation for the law of 1793. On the other hand, it was feared that these associations would augment the power of the working class as they clearly helped to organize labor. When in the 19th century the Friendly Societies developed into large, financially powerful, national organizations, not in the least because of the above-mentioned reactions to the draconian revision of the Poor Law in 1834, this fear on the part of the elites grew in intensity, and led to the call for stronger state controls.

Incidentally, these controls became necessarily stricter, since in some cases less trustworthy people realized that setting up a Friendly Society could be a profitable business. Between 1793 and 1850 not less than eighteen laws to that extent passed parliament. The most important result of this legislation was that from now on Friendly Societies had to be registered after a thorough investigation of their financial status. Only registered associations were entitled to receive the tax benefits that non-profit organizations received.[36]

Gradually the government's statutory hold on the Friendly Societies intensified, and moved, in fact, steadily towards the system of social insurance of the twentieth century. In 1874 a state committee even proposed a plan for governmental insurance: through voluntary contributions to a state controlled fund to be paid via the postal service, workers and their dependents were to be insured against the socioeconomic hardships of illness, disablement, old age, and death. A memorandum, signed by various members of the establishment of those days, listed three main advantages of such a *public system of social insurance*: (1) it would be a more efficient and effective way to administer poverty legislation; (2) rising wages would be put to use in a sensible way; (3) workers would be protected against the possible abuses of nonregistered, dishonest associations of mutual assistance. The plan was never realized but it is interesting to note the developing contours of a welfare state, albeit in the form of a collective insurance state, not of a social security state.[37] Needless to add that this proposal also serves to show how limited the idea of *laissez-faire* actually was in those days.

It was not until 1911 that the state, under the energetic leadership of the Liberal Lloyd George, entered the domain of social insurance. It did so through the National Insurance Act which set up a public system of social insurance. It was a public-private system, since the Friendly Societies were expressively incorporated in it. The decision was made that the administration of the system was to be executed not by the state and its bureaucracies, but by registered Friendly Societies. In this way public and private initiatives were merged. More than forty years later Beveridge praised this public-private partnership, yet pointed out that there were distinct disadvantages for the Friendly Societies involved: it affected their very character. "They became more official and less personal, more of insurance agencies and less of social agencies. The new responsibility affected also their numbers and their structure."[38] Smaller associations were soon wiped out, while the larger ones began to develop alongside governmental insurance schemes, albeit in a different direction: they became ordinary savings banks. The traditional *Gemeinschaft*-features faded, the bureaucratic *Gesellschaft*-character increased. In short, the Friendly Societies rationalized rapidly and attracted the common features of modernity.

It is against this background of liberalist social policy—and thus not against that of the post-war British, socialist welfare state—that one has to see the famous *Report on Social Insurance and Allied Services* (1943). Very much in the spirit of 1911 Beveridge envisaged in his design of a postwar welfare state, which he preferred to call the Social Service State, a close cooperation between the state and the private initiatives of voluntary associations. He, therefore, can hardly be seen as the "architect of the British welfare state" for which he is often held. The welfare state aspires to provide social security, that is, minimal standards of welfare and well-being for all citizens as an integral part of their citizenship. Beveridge's Social Service State rather aims at a social insurance guaranteed by the state but administered and executed by the private initiatives of voluntary associations. As to the latter, he believed that the Friendly Societies, despite their transformation after 1911, could still be used in a meaningful and efficient manner. In *Voluntary Action: A Report on Methods of Social Advance* (1948) he drew the bitter conclusion that the two National Insurance Acts of 1946—cornerstones of Labor's postwar social policy—severed the ties between public and private initiative as established in 1911: "The marriage of 1911 between the State when it entered the fields of insurance against sickness and the voluntary agencies with a hundred years' experience in this field, has been followed in 1946 by complete divorce. The State, like a Roman father, has sent the friendly societies back to live in their own house. The State is now engaged in constructing a complete and exclusive administrative machine of its own."[39] It is a centralized and bureaucratized machine, Beveridge says, and he adds this proviso, which in hindsight may have been a very wise one: "Whether any such machine can grapple with the fundamental problem of sickness benefit, of reconciling sound finance with sympathy and intimate local handling is uncertain. The government of 1911 sought the maximum of cooperation between the State and voluntary agencies in the field of social insurance. The government of 1946 has divorced the two completely."[40]

Beveridge warns here that this divorce will affect both the Friendly Societies and the State, but the State may well suffer most. In the field of social insurance it will fail to pair effective policy to the humane treatment of people, nor will it be able to avoid financial extravagances and bureaucratic formalisms. Despite the hardly concealed nostalgia vis-à-vis the brotherhood of Friendly Societies, Beveridge's warnings which were at the time not heeded by the Labor politicians who began to set up the comprehensive postwar welfare state, seem to be very timely again today. We have witnessed the rapid rise of the comprehensive welfare state in the 1960s and 1970s, and its decline again in the 1980s, and we have seen, as will be discussed later in more detail, the perverse effects of a hypertrophic, bureaucratized state that in the end stifles both the market and civil society.

Beveridge planned a system of social insurance against what he used to call: "Want, Disease, Ignorance, Squalor and Idleness."[41] What most commentators fail to see is the fact that Beveridge, unlike the postwar socialists, envisaged a Social Service State that would guarantee minimal standards for civilized living, but that at the same time would leave sufficient room for incentive, opportunity, and responsibility, enabling people to rise from these minimal standards of living to a materially and spiritually better life: "The State in organising security should not stifle incentive, opportunity, responsibility; in establishing a national minimum, it should leave room and encouragement for voluntary action by each individual to provide more than that minimum for himself and his family."[42] The socialist architects of the British welfare state did not heed Beveridge's plea for voluntarism and citizens' initiatives. They instead designed a system of comprehensive social security for all, guaranteed and financed by the state. In fact, they viewed this social security as the finishing touch of democratic citizenship. Social security to them was the essence of the fundamental social rights of all members of society. These rights would remain valid even after all socioeconomic ills had been cured eventually. This was indeed a comprehensive and utopian conception of modern citizenship: "Homes, health, education and social security, these are the birthrights," Aneurin Bevan, the postwar architect of the National Health Service, allegedly once exclaimed.[43]

Social Security and Equality

The breach between Beveridge and Bevan is indicative of the development of the welfare state, not just in Great Britain but on the continent of Europe as well. It spelled the transition of the liberal conception of social insurance to the social democratic idea of social security and of equality beyond that. Beveridge envisaged a social service state in which voluntary initiatives, in particular those of the Friendly Societies, would play a leading role in the administration and execution of the social insurance of citizens. The Labor government after the war went beyond this and envisaged a centralized and increasingly comprehensive welfare state which, as an interventionist state, would distribute and administer social security.

Moreover, all of this was ever more often viewed in terms of Marshall's theory of citizenship: equality as part and parcel of a set of social rights would herald the final step in the evolution of democratic citizenship. The welfare state was viewed from now on as a system that would distribute first and foremost equality—not merely an equality of opportunities but an equality of results. Moreover, the welfare state should provide a solid social security for all beyond a safety net of minimal social insurance, as Beveridge had envisaged. This laid the foundations for a comprehensive, that is, extensive and intensive welfare state which was lauded as the apex of democratic citizenship. The welfare state was from now on not just a system that guaranteed minimal standards for a decent and civilized living to the poor and the vulnerable of society. It instead developed into a huge, highly bureaucratized system of distribution, and, even more important, as a system of collective consumption of state-provided or subsidized services on the part of citizens. Not just the needy but all citizens were supposed to enjoy the blessings of the welfare state. Meanwhile, social research soon exposed the fact that the generally well-to-do middle classes, and thus not those who needed it most, were the main beneficiaries of the ensuing largesse of the comprehensive welfare state.

Lord Beveridge was a late representative of a socioeconomically enlightened liberalism which tried continuously to balance individual liberty and social order, voluntarism and state intervention, creativity and bureaucracy, private initiative and state planning, decentralization and centralization. Much like Lloyd George, Beveridge wanted to avoid individualistic moralism which remains always blind for the structural dimensions of socioeconomic life, without having to surrender to some sort of collectivism which diverts socioeconomic responsibilities from concrete groups and individuals to such abstract entities as "the state," "the government," "society," and so forth This is essentially the same dilemma Karl Mannheim was confronted with, when he concluded that traditionally liberal *laissez-faire* had run its course, while the totalitarian collectivism of either the extreme left (communism) or the extreme right (fascism) could not function as valid alternatives. He searched for democratic strategies of planning, which in his view had to be a substantially rational "planning for freedom."[44] Beveridge in any case wanted to transcend the nineteenth-century, liberal "nightwatcher"s state," while retaining such typically liberal values as "well-understood self-interest," "individual liberty," and "private initiative" coupled with "human dignity" and "humanitarianism."

It is interesting to observe through hindsight that both Mannheim and Beveridge who, as far as I know, never met, touched some of the grave structural weaknesses of the welfare state, and this is all the more remarkable as in those days the comprehensive welfare state was still in its infancy. And although their views cannot stand model today for alternatives to the comprehensive welfare state, their acute awareness of the structural ills of the capitalist system remains remarkable nevertheless. This is all the more so, since they tried to avoid the opposite pitfalls of a facile liberalism and an equally facile socialism.

The rationalization of care found its final and most radical expression in the social-democratic ideology of general egalitarianism. In egalitarianism, social security is seen as being complete only if a general equality of results (that is, uniformity) and the absence of any kind of elitism reign and if, in addition, this equality is structurally embedded in society. Many social democrats came to believe in the course of the 1960s that such egalitarianism could in the end only be brought about by the socialization of the means of production. They were in fact barely concealed Marxists.

The Swedish socialist Olof Palme (1927–86) was, according to his own testimony, not a Marxist, but he certainly did adhere to a radical version of social democracy. He in any case expressed his desire to go beyond social insurance and social security: "wanting to go further" it said in the title of a collection of his speeches.[45] His thoughts and policies were in line with Alva Myrdal's report on equality offered to the Swedish social democratic government in 1969. She believed the time was ripe to erect a radically egalitarian democracy, and sketched the policy measures needed to realize this utopian dream.[46] Social security and welfare, she and her fellow socialists believed, had to be radicalized into a uniform egalitarianism. Similar ideas were aired in the Netherlands by a left-wing faction of the Social Democratic party which called itself *New Left* and produced several proposals, programs, and revolutionary schemes.

We have then reached the last stage of the continuum between care-as-favor on the one end and care-as-right on the other. Care-as-right has been realized idealtypically by the comprehensive welfare state, as it emerged after World War II in most Western European nations. Among these nations Sweden and the Netherlands stood out as prime examples of a radical fashion of the welfare state—that is, until the 1980s, because in that decade it became apparent that this comprehensive welfare state had run its course. Actually, its heyday lasted not much longer than two decades. By the end of the 1970s it had already become clear to most observers that the intensive and extensive welfare state had caved in under its own weight.

Three Influential Factors

Looking back at this remarkable history, three factors in particular can be singled out as influential forces in the emergence of the comprehensive welfare state after the war. First, industrialization which in Europe began in the nineteenth century but gained real momentum after World War II in most countries, caused scores of socioeconomic problems and tensions which were condensed in the working class. Workers became an organized force of importance pressing for the official acknowledgment and actual realization of various socioeconomic rights and benefits. Even right-of-center governments proposed various socioeconomic legislations, not in the least in order to curb social unrest. Yet, the industrial revolution and the rise of the working class is not the only, and probably not even the most important factor in the rise of the welfare state.

The second, probably much more influential factor is of a demographic nature. Through industrialization standards of living improve rapidly and, in particular, life expectancies rise, not in the least through the spectacular improvements in medical cure and medical care. As a result, rapidly industrializing nations are confronted with an ever more pressing need to take care of the elderly people who live much longer than previous generations and therefore grow in number steadily. All this demands expensive health care provisions and equally expensive pension plans. In a fully modernized and industrialized society, senior citizens are no longer taken care of by their children within a family setting. As a result collective arrangements become necessary. But that is also the case because of a steady degreening of society which erodes the resources needed to finance the needed pensions. Indeed, the prime welfare state legislations are usually those dealing with collective services to the aged.[47] Health care and pensions are the items of national budgets which are generally kept least under control.

The third factor in the case of Western Europe has been World War II itself. In the Netherlands, for example, various political factions and social classes got together during the German occupation. Ironically this happened in particular in the hostage camps which the occupying Germans had set up. People who were segregated from each other before the war, were now obliged to meet physically and socially, driven together under the pressure of a common enemy. They discussed and reflected upon the kind of society they would like to see emerge after the war had ended—a society without grave socioeconomic and political inequalities and without disabling social and cultural conflicts. There was among the bourgeois and working class elites a strong common desire to reconstruct society after the war in a very fundamental manner. Beveridge's report was an example of this intellectual and political movement during the war. It served as an example for its Dutch counterpart which was published shortly after the war. It outlined a fairly comprehensive system of social insurance.

After the war, it was believed by many, irrespective of their ideological stance in the political arena, that the socioeconomic insecurities and miseries, exacerbated by the economic crisis at the end of the 1920s, had to be avoided at all social and economic costs. However, the liberal, Beveridge-like elements of this movement were soon pushed aside after the war had been concluded. Like in England, the ideological and political tone in the Netherlands was set by left-of-center social democrats. However, as in Germany, Austria, and Italy, this happened in conjunction with Christian democrats, in particular Roman Catholics who were still inspired by the papal bull *Rerum Novarum*

(1891) and tried to maintain their traditional corporatist stance.[48] Yet, Keynesian economics was believed to be the most suitable model for social and economic policies, while sociologically and public-policywise theorists like Marshall and Titmuss, rather than Beveridge and Mannheim, were celebrated as the leading thinkers concerning the rapidly expanding and intensifying welfare state.

Regressive Tendencies

We must conclude this broad survey of the rationalization of care with a warning. Rationalization as the hard core of modernization is, of course, not a unilinear process of development. Some societies lag behind, others are way ahead, or suffer from the law of the retarding lead. Again others manage to compensate their arrearage by a rapid catching-up process. However, even more intriguing is the dialectical process by which rationalization seems to summon up its very own nonrational or even antirational forces. If the comprehensive welfare state is viewed as the virtual end of the rationalization of care, it is interesting (and actually quite ironic also) to note that it gave birth to some influential regressive tendencies which seemingly counteracted the rationalizing and modernizing tendencies of the welfare state.

Members of a modern profession, to give a concrete example, demonstrate in certain respects the features of a traditional status group (*Stand*), and this is true in particular of those professions which function in the core sectors of the welfare state, like education, health care, and social security. In fact, some professions in the expanding quaternary sector resemble the traditional wealthy estates and priesthood which were exempt from toil and hard labor, and the culture of which was devoid of any trace of work ethic.[49] Whereas the feudal estates were grouped around the factor land, and the later bourgeois classes around labor and capital, these modern, welfare state professions center around the knowledge factor, or professional expertise. In a sense, they constitute an establishment with vested interests, an elite with a power and leverage that is guaranteed by the state. Many of them may verbally profess left-of-center ideas and sentiments, such as the need for solidarity and the radical redistribution of wealth for the sake of equality. Yet in reality they constitute a New Class which under the regime of a comprehensive welfare state is an establishment that serves and conserves its own interests first and foremost. They cherish their professional autonomy and dominance above all, and tend to abandon the notions of liability and responsibility which are so basic to democracy. Freidson formulated the elitist nature of this pre-modern attitude aptly, when he wrote: "it seems to be in the nature of professionally organized authority to rely on the force and prerogatives of its official status rather than to undertake the wearisome effort of persuading and demonstrating."[50]

It stands to reason that professionals thus lost touch with democratic civil society and acquired the attitudes and habits of state officials. Professionals and civil servants share common interests. On-the-rebound citizens in civil society often turn away from these professionals, and develop nonprofessional, informal forms of care. Thus, in the heyday of the comprehensive welfare state (the 1960s and 1970s) self-help and mutual aid groups emerged in which people tried to take care of certain, usually immaterial (psycho-social) problems without the help and interference of professionals. In these groups bureaucratic formalism was usually avoided and replaced by face-to-face relations, which were more often than not nonrational or even irrational. This is not to say, however, that they were philanthropic or altruistic. The so-called helper principle, for instance, was discovered soon as a therapeutic instrument: in helping others to overcome a certain problem one is allegedly enabled to come to grips with one's own problems. Alcoholics Anonymous has from early on applied this therapy.[51] Even if such self-help and mutual aid groups developed into relatively large and formal organizations, the principle of small scale, often labeled "human scale," and of mutual relations remained at their core. Next to Alcoholics Anonymous the "buddy system" in the nonprofessional, informal care of AIDS patients is a recent example, even though it has kept a low profile in terms of formal organization.

The reemergence of such self-help and mutual aid groups is in the context of a comprehensive welfare state perhaps surprising on first sight. But it can be interpreted in part also as a reaction to the rationalization and formalization of professionalized and bureaucratized care in the welfare state. In a sense, they seem to fill up the emotional gap that rationalization and profesionalization have left in the welfare state.

There are apparently some deep, underlying, historical structures at work here.[52] Puritan dissenters emancipated themselves from the Catholic and Anglican clerics (in a sense the leading "professionals" of the premodern and early modern world) by organizing themselves outside the established "churches" in "sects," where they learned to take care of each other and themselves. The rationalists of the Enlightenment, in a sense the secularized successors of the Puritans, in particular the Liberals, voiced their strong opposition against statutory care of the poor under the regime of the Poor Law, and applauded the private, mutual aid of the Friendly Societies. Likewise, the self-help and mutual aid groups that emerged under the regime of the welfare state, opposed in their turn the professionally rational dominance of state regulated and subsidized care and welfare.

This reemergence of self-help is, in a sense, a sort of regressive tendency in the evolution of care. The self-help movement has often been described as a left-of-center, "progressive" movement, just as the guru of anti-professionalism, Ivan Illich, was internationally applauded as a "progressive" and "left-of-center" thinker and activist. This is quite erroneous and deceptive to boot, because self-help and mutual aid are, in actual fact, quite traditional, informal and non-rational—and in this sense "regressive"—approaches to the dispensation of care. Illich too was not very progressive in his approach. With his anti-professionalist theories he meant to undermine the interests and idcological ideas of most of the progressive representatives of the New Class who, as we saw, have always been inclined to heed carefully their own professional dominance first and foremost.

In short, as to rationalization the comprehensive welfare state demonstrated derationalizing, regressive tendencies. This was quite apparent as far as knowledge was concerned. The knowledge of most care and welfare professionals was often expressed, verbally and in writing, in an abstract and esoteric argot which managed to alienate their clients progressively. Modern knowledge is necessarily specialized knowledge, expressed in a necessarily technical and abstract jargon. On the level of advanced technology (such as aeronautics, nuclear physics, astronomy, or higher information sciences) people are willing to accept incomprehensible jargon, but when their daily lives in such sectors as education, health and social security, are involved, they demand, of course, clear and understandable language. Thus, while the growth of professionalism in the welfare state gave rise to often highly abstract and esoteric knowledge and language, the call for "clear," "concrete," "understandable" knowledge and language grew louder and louder.

Not surprisingly, also paramedical therapies, often couched in premodern, magical forms of thought and scores of esoteric philosophies gained popularity while the official medical world, stimulated and legitimated by the welfare state, continued to expand and intensify its arcane professionalism.

All of this is actually part of a much more general call for derationalization, a call for experiential and emotionally satisfying knowledge at the expense of theoretical, abstract, cognitive ideas and concepts. It is comparable to religious fundamentalism which abhors abstract theology and wants to return to the existentially and emotionally rewarding experience of faith. If the word "fundamentalism" had not been abused so much, one could speak of "cognitive fundamentalism."

We observe here how the welfare state, particularly the intensive and extensive welfare state, summons its own opposition. It is, in other words, basically an ambiguous phenomenon. This conclusion deserves closer scrutiny.

Notes

1. See Abram de Swaan, *In Care of the State: Health Care, Education and Welfare in Europe and the USA in the Modern Era* (Cambridge, UK: Polity Press, 1988).
2. Robert Whalen, *The Corrosion of Charity: From Moral Renewal to Contract Culture* (London: The Institute of Economic Affairs Health and Welfare Unit, 1996). Choice in Welfare Series no. 29.
3. Marc Bloch, *Feudal Society*, volume 1: "The Growth of Ties of Dependence," translated by L.A. Manyon, (Chicago: University of Chicago Press; London: Routledge and Kegan Paul, 1970, 8th ed.). See, in particular, part 4: "The Ties between Man and Man: Vassalage and the Fief," pp. 145–281.
4. At the end of the 1970s I collaborated with a colleague in a research project within the area of service clubs. We focused in particular upon a comparison of these voluntary associations in the United States and in the comprehensive welfare state setting of Sweden and the Netherlands. It was very obvious that in the heyday of the extensive and intensive welfare state in Europe such service clubs could not function properly, simply because service to the community was considered to be a statutory task of the state. As a result, they could only function as social spaces for networking and acquisition of social prestige. I reported on this in a joined Dutch publication: H. P. M. Adriaansens, A. C. Zijderveld, *Vrijwillig initiatief en de verzorgingsstaat* (Voluntary initiatives and the welfare state), (Deventer: Van Loghum Slaterus, 1981), See chapter 5: "Service clubs in de verzorgingsstaat" (Service clubs in the welfare state), pp. 129–43.
5. Ernest W. McDonnell, *The Beguines and Beghards in Medieval Culture: With Special Emphasis on the Belgian Scene* (New Brunswick, NJ: Rutgers University Press, 1954)
6. Cf. J.J.C.B. Bremer, *De ziekenhuispatiënt*, (Nijmegen: Dekker and Van de Vegt, 1964), p. 78.
7. Cf. Hansfried Kellner, Frank W. Heuberger (eds.), *Hidden Technocrats: The New Class and New Capitalism* (New Brunswick, NJ: Transaction Publishers, 1992). For "Knowledge Class" see Peter L. Berger, *The Capitalist Revolution* (New York: Basic Books, 1986), pp. 66–70.
8. Cf. Ivan Illich, "Disabling Professions", Ivan Illich, et al. (eds.), *Disabling Professions* (New York: Marion Boyars Publishers, [1977]1992), pp. 11–40.
9. Cf. Marc Bloch, *Feudal Society*, volume 1, part 1: "The Environment: The Last Invasions", pp. 3-58. Also Geoffrey Barraclough, *The Crucible of Europe: The Ninth and Tenth Centuries in European History* (Berkeley and Los Angeles:

University of California Press, 1976), chapter 3: "The decline and fall of the Carolingian Empire," pp. 54–73; and chapter 4: "The impact of invasion," pp. 74–83.

10. Bloch, *Feudal Society*, volume 1, part 3: "The Ties between Man and Man: Kinship," pp. 123–44.
11. Jean Froissart, *Chronicles,* translated by G. Brereton (London: Penguin [c. 1400]1979), pp. 211–30.
12. Jean-Louis Goglin, *Les misérables dans l'Occident médiéval* (Paris: Éditions du Seuil, 1976).
13. J.J.C.B. Bremer, *De ziekenhuispatiënt*, p. 71. Bremer makes a pertinent observation: "Just as the hospital patient today reaches his bed by way of the administration office and the bathtub, the medieval patient had to pass the confession box" [my translation].
14. Cf. T. H. Marshall, *Class, Citizenship and Social Development* (Chicago: The University of Chicago Press [1963]1977), p. 87.
15. Cf. A. de Swaan, *In Care of the State.*
16. Maurice Bruce, *The Coming of the Welfare State* (London: Batsford [1961]1968; rev. 4th ed.), p. 36.
17. Christopher Hill, *The Century of Revolution, 1603–1714* (London: Cardinal, [1961]1974), p. 33.
18. M. Bruce, *The Coming of the Welfare State*, p. 44.
19. W. Beveridge, *Voluntary Action: A Report on Methods of Social Advance* (London: His Majesty's Stationary Office [1942]1948), p. 128.
20. Richard Niebuhr, *The Social Sources of Denominationalism* (New York: Meridian Books, The World Publishing Company, [1929]1962; 6th ed.), p. 105. Niebuhr believes that this gospel has been part of the bourgeoisification of Puritanism: "Here [i.e., in the Middle Class] the gospel of self-help has excluded all remnants of that belief in fatality which formed the foundation of Puritan heroism."
21. C. Hill, *The Century of Revolution*, p. 78.
22. M. Bruce, *The Coming of the Welfare State*, p. 78.
23. Cf. Hill, *The Century of Revolution*, p. 121ff.
24. See the interesting argument in Arthur J. Taylor, *Laissez-faire and State Intervention in Nineteenth-century Britain* (London: Macmillan, [1972]1978).
25. M. Bruce, *The Coming of the Welfare State*, p. 94.
26. See Michael Ignatieff, *A Just Measure of Pain: The Penitentiary in the Industrial Revolution 1750–1850* (London: Penguin Books, [1978]1989).
27. M. Bruce, *The Coming of the Welfare State*, p. 95f.
28. Ibid., p. 98.
29. T.H. Marshall, *Class, Citizenship and Social Development*, p. 88.
30. W. Beveridge, *Voluntary Action*, p. 127.
31. M. Bruce, *The Coming of the Welfare State*, p. 122.
32. W. Beveridge, *Voluntary Action*, p. 23.
33. Alfred H. Katz, Eugene I. Bender, "Self-help Groups in Western Society. History and Prospects," *Journal of Applied Behavioral Science* (1976), 12(3): 265–82.
34. W. Beveridge, *Voluntary Action*, p. 21.
35. Ibid., p. 60.
36. Ibid., p. 65f.
37. Ibid., p. 66f.
38. Ibid., p. 78f.
39. Ibid., p. 80f.
40. Ibid., p. 83.

41. W. Beveridge, *Social Insurance and Allied Services*, p. 6.
42. Ibid., p. 6f.
43. A.S.A. Briggs, "The Welfare State in Historical Perspective," *Archive Européenne de la Sociologie* (1961) 2: 227.
44. Karl Mannheim, *Man and Society in an Age of Reconstruction* (London: Routledge and Kegan Paul [1940]1960), p. 379: "planning for freedom is the only logical form of freedom which remains."
45. Gunnar Heckscher, *The Welfare State and Beyond: Success and Problems in Scandinavia* (Minneapolis: University of Minnesota Press, 1984), p. 250. When in the 1970s economic growth declined sharply and the previously seemingly unlimited resources appeared to be very limited indeed, the architects and defenders of the Swedish comprehensive welfare state were in problems. Heckscher quotes a remark by Palme which is rather characteristic of his state of mind: "In an unguarded moment Olof Palme said the 'realities are our most dangerous enemy,'" ibid., p. 236.
46. Alva Myrdal, *Equality*, abridged version translated by Roger Lind (Stockholm: Prisma, [1969]1971).
47. This was strongly emphasized by Harold L. Wilensky, *The Welfare State and Equality: Structural and Ideological Roots of Public Expenditures* (Berkeley and Los Angeles: University of California Press, 1975), p. 47f.: "If there is one source of welfare spending that is most powerful—a single proximate cause—it is the proportion of old people in the population. The welfare state is a symbol of the aged in modern society, both dependent and independent, a minority of strategic importance in public spending."
48. See Kees van Kersbergen, *Social Capitalism: A Study of Christian Democracy and the Welfare State* (New York: Routledge, 1995). The author focuses primarily on the social philosophy of Roman Catholicism.
49. See Helmuth Schelsky, *Die Arbeit tun die Anderen. Klassenkampf und Priesterherrschaft der Intellektuellen* (Work is done by others: Class conflict and priest power of intellectuals) (Opladen: Westdeutscher Verlag, 1975).
50. Eliot Freidson, *Professional Dominance: The Social Structure of Medical Care* (New York: Atherton [1970]1977), p. 235.
51. Frank Riessman, "The 'Helper' Therapy Principle," *Social Work* (1965) 10(2): 27–32.
52. Alfred H. Katz and Eugene I. Bender, "Self-help Groups in Western Society: History and Prospects," *Journal of Applied Behavioral Science* (1976) 12(3): 265–82.

2

An Ambiguous Project

The Initial Dream

Looking at the welfare state through hindsight, it can hardly be denied that there is an element of tragedy in its development after World War II. Tragedy is the deeply human phenomenon that the sublime is sought and tried for by all means possible, yet the opposite of this lofty and praiseworthy aim is realized unconsciously as in an unintended consequence. A Dutch theologian and philosopher once defined tragedy aptly and succinctly as the high endeavor which frustrates itself, which by a dark necessity turns against itself.[1]

After several decades of existence it has been nearly forgotten that during the reconstruction period immediately after World War II the welfare state was meant as a *moral* project, as it actually professed to realize the three basic values of the French Revolution. Liberty and equality, notoriously at odds with each other (if one wants to foster the one, the other has to be curbed), were to be couched in and borne by solidarity. However, particularly the advanced (intensive and extensive) welfare states in Western Europe demonstrated soon that the bureaucratic administration of a highly centralized state curbed the liberties fostered by democratic societies, while new forms of inequality and dependence emerged, and soon enough developed into structural components of the increasingly comprehensive welfare state.

As to solidarity, citizens were made to believe initially that the sharply progressive tax system and the various premiums and contributions were meant to redistribute wealth, thereby banning uncivilized destitution, poverty, and social exclusion. But soon after the comprehensive welfare state had become a fact of daily life, it became hard to envisage the often sharply progressive direct and indirect taxes and excises as realizations of one's solidarity with fellow citizens who for reasons outside their guilt lived in materially dire circumstances. In the comprehensive welfare state, solidarity acquired an exceedingly abstract character. Likewise, the recipients of state succor were generally not aware of any solidarity on the part of their more fortunate fellow citizens. This succor, they were being told time and again by welfare professionals and state administrators, was the realization of their basic social right of citizenship. They were legally and in some countries even constitutionally entitled to it. In short, the lofty ideals of the French Revolution lost much of their initial democratic luster.

In addition the law of rising expectations began to wreak havoc on the welfare state also, posing it for ever larger and costlier public expenditures. Likewise, poverty, it was discovered in due time, is not an absolute but a relative phenomenon, related to the general level of prosperity of a society. The destitution and misery of nineteenth-century poverty was banned, but a new kind of poverty appeared to be persistent: the exclusion from the world of productive labor and from the opportunities to participate fully in social and cultural life. This new brand of poverty, already labeled "New Poverty," was concentrated in particular in special categories of people, such as single parents, senior citizens, ethnic minorities, undocumented migrants, the long-term unemployed, and the unemployable.

As to unemployment, the lofty aim of full employment, once a cornerstone of the welfare state, proved to be unattainable within the framework of an ever more extensive and intensive welfare state. In fact, unemployment which was low in the 1960s, did rise in most Western European countries steadily in the course of the 1970s and early 1980s, and this happened ironically on par with the expansion of the welfare state. Scores of economic and socioscientific theories and analyses have tried to explain these contradictory facts, few of which focused on the comprehensive welfare state itself as the most probable cause of these social and economic ills. In any case, these ills contributed to the gradual undermining of the moral project of a caring state.

Even foes of the welfare state ought to acknowledge its inherent, initial decency. One should not forget that the comprehensive welfare state emerged in Europe, a continent in which equality and liberty have always been at odds with the dominant class structures of society. This was, of course, acerbated by the Industrial Revolution in the nineteenth century. Those in favor of democracy, which in essence is the ideal of a civilized society based upon liberty, equality, and solidarity, ought to applaud the welfare state as an inherently decent and civil project. There is, of course, nothing wrong with an ideal which envisages a society in which there is a structurally, state-guaranteed set of equal opportunities in the crucial and often vulnerable sectors of human life, namely work, health, education, housing, and old age. Illness, illiteracy, bad housing, unemployment and a miserable old age are the scourges of an uncivilized society for which there ought to be no room in a democracy.

But, as most welfare states of Western Europe have demonstrated in the 1960s, 1970s, and1980s, things went dramatically wrong. In fact, in many respects the very opposite of this praiseworthy ideal was reached. The intensive and extensive welfare state was wrought with multiple ambiguities which in the 1980s led to its decline, or better still, its fundamental transformation.

In 1959 Gunnar Myrdal argued that the then already emerging etatism of the incipient welfare state was to be viewed as a necessary transition towards a society in which the distribution of welfare would lead to a *welfare culture* borne and dispensed by local authorities and scores of societal organizations, run by free and actively involved citizens. It is a remarkable variation of the Leninist notion of the gradual withering away of the state as a bourgeois institution. The welfare state, he prophesied in a rather utopian mood, would soon develop into the very opposite of an interventionist state leading citizens on a road to serfdom. On the contrary, he believed, the power of the centralized state would eventually diminish in favor of lower authorities, such as urban governments, and societal organizations.[2] Four decades later we know Myrdal was very wrong. The bureaucrats and the professionals of the well established welfare state did not willingly forsake their power and particular interests. Ordinary citizens too got used to the "welfare culture," while expecting from the state and its officials ever more legislative initiatives and in particular subsidies, which had to cater generously to their well-being, their particularistic interests, and their ever rising expectations. Needless to add, scores of rules and regulations were tied to this welfare largesse, weaving a complex web of a Tocquevillean, and thus benign, yet ever stricter control. Until the oil crises in the mid-1970s the sky seemed, to all involved, the limit. Politicians deemed it expedient to give in to the many faceted demands all the time, adding steadily to a public debt that the generations after them had to pay off.

All this indicates that the welfare state, particularly as it came into shape in Western Europe after World War II, appears to have been a rather ambiguous phenomenon. It makes sense to discuss the main ambiguities, as they throw light upon both the organizational and institutional dimensions of the welfare state, and upon its inherent weaknesses as well.

Centralized State and Civil Society

It is nowadays a piece of common political wisdom that a strong civil society consisting of organizations that possess a high degree of autonomy vis-à-vis the state, constitutes the most fundamental precondition for a vital democracy. It was more than just symbolic that in communist Poland *Solidarnocs* and its fight for a trade union that stands independent vis-à-vis the totalitarian state, heralded the beginning of the end of the communist reign in Central and Eastern Europe. Thus, in a sense the velvet revolution of 1989 started from within civil society. In communism it is not only the market which is kept under state control through a very strict and top-down planning, but society too is kept under etatist tutelage.

In totalitarian societies which are not socialist or communist, the central state may favor capitalism and a free market, but is bent to keep societal organizations under the strict control of the central apparatus. In actual fact, the nondemocratric state renders them into extension pieces of its heavy-handed and top-down power. Not just the trade unions, if they do develop at all, also religious, educational, youth, artistic, and leisure organizations—often called "corporations"—are kept under close scrutiny and the tutelage of the central government. As in radically socialist countries, a civil society of free organizations, so essential to a truly democratic polity, does not exist in such fascist-corporatist systems.

It stands to reason that the destruction of civil society gives rise to a particular brand of collectivism which is at the same time a brand of individualism. Individuals are grouped together in state-organized collecitivities in which they are controlled, and expected to dispense the ideas, feelings and acts favored by the central state and voiced by the single party. Within these often rather anomic collectivities individuals are more often than not rather isolated atoms, subjected to a pervasive lack of mutual trust. In fact, in a totalitarian, either fascist or radically socialist society one is, if it comes to trust and mutual reliability, on one's own. In other words, what is called *social capital* is very low, if not absent, in a totalitarian system.[3]

In such a system the state is able to reach and control individual citizens—subjects rather—directly, without any mediation. Tocqueville,

Durkheim, and Weber have, each in their own particular ways, discussed the role of civil society in democracy in terms of mediating, or intermediary structures. Ever since, mediating structures have indeed been the crucial components of any sociological theory of democracy. The strength of a democratic civil society rests, according to this theory, in structures—organizations, institutions—which have a large degree of autonomy vis-à-vis the state, as well as the individual citizens. They function, as it were, as buffers between state and citizens, softening the power of the former and the influence of particular interests and demands of the latter. Through mediating structures power is, as it were, dampened and thereby society is indeed civilized. Or, to phrase it differently, mediating structures render power legitimate, transforming power into authority.[4]

A comprehensive welfare state, such as evolved in most Western European nations after World War II, was designed and has always been intended as a democratic system. There is in Western European welfare states no totalitarian etatism, dictated by a single party, and its citizens do possess constitutionally grounded civil, political, and in some cases even social rights. But the organizations of civil society which are independent, if not autonomous vis-à-vis the state *de jure*, usually develop into extension pieces of the central state *de facto*. They surrender important portions of their independence and autonomy the moment the welfare state system emerges and develops into a comprehensive behemoth. This causes the weakening of civil society and the mediating structures in it. Power is gradually delegitimated and thus authority is weakened. All this, needless to add, negatively affects the civic spirit of the citizens. In other words, the comprehensive welfare state puts democracy under a heavy strain, not just economically and politically, but also socially, culturally, and morally.

The etatism of the welfare state is unlike totalitarian etatism—not top-down but rather bottom-up, as it is in fact called for and stimulated by the organizations in civil society and in particular, as we saw before, by the care professionals in the fields of health, education and welfare. They are joined in their etatist orientation by bureaucrats, politicians, and most social scientists.

There are, in particular, two processes which have fostered this curious bottom-up etatism of the comprehensive welfare state. First, the central government in an extensive and intensive welfare state is called upon to finance scores of activities in civil society, causing the spectacular rise of public spending, mainly in the form of state subsidies and tax facilities for the organizations in the public realm but often in the private realm also, as in the case of failing industrial corporations. It stands to reason that etatist strings in the form of controls, rules, and regulations are being attached to these subsidies. Consequently, it is the central government that sets the agenda for these legally independent but financially dependent organizations.

Second, particularly in the ever-expanding quaternary sector welfare services are increasingly set up and executed by professionals who gradually push aside the well-meaning and morally motivated amateur volunteers of the days of charity. These care professionals are stakeholders in the health, education and welfare business, and prefer the power of a firmly centralized state above the often informal and formerly authoritarian influence of the boards of the organizations that employ them. Their sociopolitical clout, the level of their salaries and the certification of their diplomas are in a welfare state guaranteed primarily by the central administration and its bureaucracies. Their socioeconomic and political orientation, therefore, focuses first and foremost upon the central state, the central administration and its bureaucracies, and thus not on civil society in which they are supposed to operate primarily.

Naturally, these professionals are joined in their etatist orientation by most bureaucrats and politicians, since they too are prime stakeholders in the welfare business. Needless to add it is the social scientists, psychologists, and sociologists in the first place, who generally receive relatively large research funds from the state bureaucracies. In particular the state ministries of health, education, and welfare are used to commission socio-scientific research, if alone to legitimate the policy decisions they have made or intend to make.

It is usually believed that the market, in particular big business, is adverse to these etatist developments of the welfare state. That is not entirely correct. Demands for financial support (subsidies) did not solely come from civil society, in particular its quaternary sector, but also from the market, in particular its corporate components. When, for instance, industries like ship building, textile industry, or shoemaking declined due to fierce global competitions from countries with cheaper labor, the state was more or less forced politically to intervene financially. Astronomic amounts of public money have been channeled into industrial branches which were from the start unfit to survive global competitions, or have become obsolete altogether, as in the case of coal mining. These subsidies, bails, and forfeits too, as is often forgotten in the private sector, have been part and parcel of welfare state largesse. From the start the fight against unemployment has been one of the major projects of the welfare state. As a result, the central government was time and again put under heavy pressure by necessitous branches of business which, in conjunction with trade unions, used the threat of massive lay-offs as an argument addressed to the central state to intervene financially. These pressures often came close to extortion.

The result of all this was, of course, that the welfare state led to a rapid expansion of the central administration and its bureaucracies, whereas both the market and civil society maneuvered itself into a position of dependence upon this centralized, bureaucratized megastructure. As a result, not just the market, as is repeated time and again by the economic critics of the welfare state, but civil society itself began to lose its stamina, its vitality, and its much needed flexibility. As a result nations with a comprehensive welfare state began to suffer the sociocultural and economic fate of totalitarian societies, the huge difference being though that its citizens enjoyed freedom and legally grounded civil, political, and social rights—the alleged three cornerstones of democratic citizenship.

This is indeed a curious ambiguity. Myrdal was right, the welfare state as such is not a road to totalitarian serfdom. But he was mistaken in believing that its etatism and centralization, both intensely detrimental to the vitality of a civil society of free organizations, would remain a transitory phase, and evolve eventually into a situation in which the central state would fulfill but a marginal role and civil society would fully blossom and prosper, as it should in a true democracy. The decades following the appearance of his *Beyond the Welfare State* (1959) have fully falsified Myrdal's utopian prediction. A fully fledged welfare state may constitutionally still be democratic, but because of the ever increasing demands and steadily rising expectations from below, it will develop well-nigh inevitably into a comprehensive megastructure the regulations and controls of which will then penetrate deeply into the market and civil society.

Horizontalism and Verticalism

It remains a puzzling question why and how several welfare states in Western Europe developed as rapidly and as radically as they actually did after World War II. Certainly in comparison to the welfare state arrangements in most parts of the United States, the welfare states of

Western Europe grew in a relatively short period of time (between 1950 and 1980) into remarkably intensive and extensive megastructures. There are, of course, on the Western European continent various differences due to rather different historical and national developments. Yet, compared collectively to the situation in the United States, most European welfare states exhibit a remarkable degree of comprehensiveness.

An important part of the answer is the fact that in most Western European countries there is traditionally an ambiguous relationship between horizontal and vertical structures, the latter fostering the emergence of welfare state arrangements which are set-up, administrated and funded primarily, although never exclusively, by the central administration in a vertical, top-down fashion. This needs further explanation.

One of the macrostructural characteristics of American society is, notwithstanding the admittedly great variety of the individual states, the traditional emphasis upon local governments and the traditional practice of scores of voluntary associations. Since Tocqueville, Europeans have been struck by the fact that between individual American citizens and their nuclear families on the one hand and the state, particularly the federal state, on the other, scores of mediating structures— voluntary associations first and foremost—are at work. They constitute a solid civil society made up, so to say, of horizontal layers that buffer the power of the state and its controls and regulations. In fact, the very founders of the nation were Protestant dissenters who had rejected and left behind the strongly verticalist, top-down Anglican state-church and the equally top-down absolutism of the monarchy. Lately the strength and vigor of America's civil society is much debated. The question is, if indeed this picture of a predominantly horizontally structured society of voluntary associations is still correct.[5] If not, this would indeed be a historical breach, and a seminal transformation of a society which as of old has been one with strong horizontal and weak vertical structures. However, the idea of a strong, centralized government trying to function as an active and intervening welfare state, administered by the federal government in Washington DC, as in the New Deal of Roosevelt or the Great Society of Johnson, has never been embraced wholeheartedly by the majority of American citizens. It runs counter to what could be called a Culture of Horizontalism.

In comparison, the Netherlands is an interesting case, since it presented traditionally a curious mixture of horizontalism and verticalism, which in a way prepared the road to a rather radical welfare state in which verticalism superseded horizontalism. Prior to 1960, when the present welfare state began to develop and expand rapidly, there was a massive civil society consisting of scores of mainly voluntary associations and numerable organizations devoted to the welfare of Dutch citizens. The bulk of these organizations and associations were founded upon worldviews—not just religious worldviews, such as Roman Catholicism, Orthodox, and Liberal Protestantism, but also secular worldviews, such as socialism and liberalism, the last two often called "neutral" or "humanistic" in distinction to their religious counterparts. Thus, various sectors of society, such as education, health care, media, trade unions, employers' associations, political parties, and even sport and leisure organizations, including student unions at the universities, were, and to a certain degree still are, set up separately according to worldview. In this respect, Dutch society possesses a massively corporatist tradition. There are still today Catholic, Protestant and "Neutral" schools and universities, hospitals, and trade unions. Recently the Muslims, descendants mainly of Turkish and Moroccan "guest workers" of the 1960s, are growing in numbers and influence. They set up their own Islamic primary schools, which together with a Muslim broadcasting corporation and other Muslim organizations constitute the beginning of a small Muslim "nation" within Dutch society.

This curious system of minority organization, it should be borne in mind, is not an ecclesiastic but a societal phenomenon. Although the Roman Catholic Church in particular kept a close watch over Catholic organizations, it did not administer them, nor were they financed by the church. It has been and still is the central state which is responsible for an equitable funding of the various confessional and humanist-neutral organizations and institutions in civil society. It was decided by the parliament in 1917, after a rather long conflict—a fierce cultural war indeed—about the question of whether the state should subsidize confessional and neutral education equally (the Catholics and Protestants being pro, the socialists and liberals con), that all educational institutions were to be subsidized equally by the state. This pacification principle put in the constitution after 1917, was then extended to the equal treatment by the state of all organizations based upon religious or secular worldviews. The constitutional principle of the separation of state and church was upheld, but through its often lavish subsidies to which, of course, scores of regulations and controls were tied, the state got a top-down, vertical hold on much of Dutch civil society.

This verticalist system has become called *pillarization*, since these structures based upon worldview would run perpendicularly through the different classes of society. In fact, people would identify with their worldview-organizations first and with their classes next. Workers were divided into Protestant, Catholic, and socialist trade unions.

The pillars were vertical in another sense also. Until the 1960s, these organizations were ruled top-down by a relatively small elite of prominent men who wielded their authority in an authoritarian manner. Prior to the 1960s people looked up to them, listened to them, obeyed them. In fact, these pillarized elites transcended the often fierce differences of worldview in society, and met each other regularly, informally and in a gentlmanly manner in order to discuss the demarcation of their respective interests. They discussed in particular various political affairs, prepared coalition governments, and prearranged important political decisions, to be passed in parliament. It reminded opponents of pillarization of the Italian Mafia. In any case, also in this patrimonial sense, pillarization was a vertical top-down structure. It gave Dutch corporatism a very special character and flavor because after all the call for the top-down interventions came from organizations within civil society.

The welfare state, which emerged in the 1950s and expanded radically after 1960, made full use of these vertical, pillarized structures. The central government, always by necessity the result of coalitions of various parties, since no pillar could obtain an electoral majority, employed these vertical pillarized structures as the conductors of its welfare state activities and interventions. This was, of course, facilitated, when after 1960 secularization set in rather rapidly which in a sense defundamentalized the respective worldviews, rendering them into quite modern, generalized and vague organizational cultures, while it did not destroy the system of pillarization as such. On the contrary, until today there are still Catholic, Protestant, and humanist schools, hospitals, universities, television, and broadcasting corporations, and as mentioned earlier the Muslims growing in number have begun to pillarize also. Meanwhile, the central state finances through subsidies and tax benefits, and orchestrates with rules and regulations the main welfare activities of these organizations. The result is a curious mixture of horizontalism and verticalism which gives the Dutch welfare state an equally curious, ambiguous character.

Sweden's welfare state is in many respects quite different from the Dutch but the two have the comprehensivenss of their respective welfare states in common. The traditional verticalism of Sweden is historically determined by the fact that there is in Sweden, despite secularization and modernization, no constitutional separation of church and state. The Lutheran church is the established state church. Like in Holland, here too modernization and secularization have de-fundamentalized the verticalism that a state church brings about, while the situation has structurally not changed at all, since the Lutheran church is still the officially established church. As in Holland, horizontalism was paired to verticalism, and the latter became the more prominent with the emergence of the welfare state which could easily be set up along the vertical lines of the state church.

In a sense, the same happened in Great Britain, the difference being that traditionally several dissenting Protestants possessed their own voluntary organizations outside the power and jurisdiction of the Anglican state-church. Many of them left in the 17th century and set up their horizontalist colony on the North American continent. All this led eventually to a quite different type of mixture of horizontalism and verticalism, and thus to a different type of welfare state.

On the North American continent Québec stands out as an example of a comprehensive welfare state which has put into effect its strong tradition of Catholicism and Catholic corporatism. It led to a curious and ambiguous mixture of verticalism and horizontalism.

It stands to reason that when the welfare state declines or is curbed for whatever reasons, as has happened everywhere in Western Europe after 1980, verticalism will decline in favor of horizontalism. It entails necessarily a strengthening of civil society and a weakening of the central administration.

Values and Functions

The previous ambiguities were predominantly of a socio-structural nature. There is, however, also a set of cultural ambiguities which are at play in a less visible, yet no less influential manner. The extensive and intensive welfare state grew into a megastructure whose redistributing, regulating, and controlling *functions* became so obvious and taken-for-granted, that the people involved—citizens, politicians, bureaucrats, and welfare professionals—lost sight of the fact that pertinent and forceful *values* stood at its foundations. The ever-expanding bureaucracy of the comprehensive welfare state suggested that this megastructure was a value-free and amoral set of functions. This may be the case, since the comprehensive welfare state has come about. But if one takes cognizance of the ideas of some of the founding fathers of the various welfare states, it becomes obvious that initially values did play quite an influential role.

Admittedly, often enough reasons of state, *Staatsraison*, rather than religious or humanist values were prominent when politicians set out to design legal arrangements of social insurance and social security. Bismarck, as is often related in this context, saw his *Sozialstaat* as an instrument to curb the unrest and weaken the potentially revolutionary force of the working class. However, most European welfare states developed fully after World War II, and they were designed with the still lively memories of the dire miseries of the years of crisis after 1929 and the years of material and immaterial destruction during the war of 1939–45 in mind. The welfare state was part of the utopian, postwar dream to reconstruct the market and civil society in such a way that democracy could be founded upon both affluence and justice.

Lord Beveridge stands out as an example of this dream. If he was not really, as has been argued before, the architect of the British welfare state, as he is often presented, his utopian vision did have a strong resonance in the Western world. His famous *Report on Social Insurance and Allied Services* (1943) reads as a technocratic, legalistic, and rather bureaucratic exercise of social planning. But underneath it and more explicitly in other publications, such as the treatise on *Voluntary Action* (1948) and the collected essays and speeches in *Why I am a Liberal* (1946), some very basic, humanist values were obviously at work in his mind. He envisaged a society in which all citizens would be insured against what he called the five scourges of humanity: "Want, Disease, Ignorance, Squalor and Idleness." He added at the same time that the social service arrangements for the prevention of these calamities were to be guaranteed and, where and when needed, funded by the state. However, he proposed also that these services were to be administered and executed by societal organizations. As to the latter, it has to be said once more, voluntary action in the context of voluntary associations (in Great Britain's case the Friendly Societies in the first place) was and remained crucial. He insisted upon this point, lest society and the market be stifled and suffocated by an all-embracing, regulating and controlling central and bureaucratic government. What he envisioned was, of course, a welfare state which would avert the five scourges of humanity, but maintained at the same time the *liberty* which a civil society needs in order to remain truly democratic, and which the market needs in order to function properly.

It stands to reason that social democrats would emphasize quite a different set of values in their conception of the welfare state. To them the five scourges of humanity had a common cause in basic and structurally determined, predominantly socioeconomic inequalities. The central value of their vision was and remained *equality*, to be guaranteed by a central government whose main task it was to conduct and control the *planning* of the market and civil society.[6] The welfare state, in this vision, is a centralized megastructure which curbs the social and particular economic liberties that classical capitalism has always demanded. It ought to redistribute public and private wealth in order to reduce the socioeconomic inequalities inherent to the capitalist mode of production. But as we have witnessed in the 1960s and 1970s planning in the context of a comprehensive welfare state evolved well-nigh autonomously into a technocratic, very bureaucratic control, devoid of deeper, religious or humanist values, promoting a mindless kind of functionalism, and, what is worse, a debilitating egalitarianism. It unintentionally enlarged the regulating and controlling power of the state exponentially, at the expense, of course, of the market and civil society.

Meanwhile, with the expansion and intensification of the welfare state the original values of liberty and equality evaporated, grew into clichés, ideological commonplaces of respectively liberalism and socialism. In the end, these clichés came down to a superficial juxtaposition of a free market vis-à-vis a planned economy which, it stands to reason, had to end up in the middle. It was called a "mixed economy." In fact, these ideologies were absorbed and neutralized by the welfare state and its functionalism. Not surprisingly, they failed to inspire bureaucrats, administrators, and politicians, let alone businessmen and ordinary citizens. The dreary, technocratic functionalism that was the result of all of this heralded indeed the end of ideology and the end of history, albeit in a different sense than the authors of two celebrated books on the subject had in mind.[7]

The welfare state, in a sense the grand project of a late Enlightenment, is, as we saw before, also founded upon the third value that has driven the Western world ever since the French Revolution: brotherhood, or perhaps better, *solidarity*. Initially this value inspired people as class solidarity, i.e., as bourgeois solidarity, or workers' solidarity. Within the Christian democratic frame of reference solidarity was not interpreted in terms of classes and class conflicts, but rather in terms of religiously inspired organizations and their related sense of consensual community. However, within the framework of the expanding welfare state solidarity became much less concrete. In fact, citizens are being told in rather abstract argot that public and private wealth is to be redistributed by the welfare state in order to reduce socioeconomic and political inequalities. But the more complex and bureaucratic this welfare state grew, the less convincing the solidarity argument became. In fact, the legitimacy of the sharply progressive taxes and the multiple direct and indirect excises, in particular the social insurance payments and social security premiums, which the comprehensive state imposed on citizens and corporations, declined proportionately and rapidly. As was said before, it took quite a bit of imagination to accept emotionally the long list of deductions on one's monthly paycheck as one's personal contribution to the value of solidarity with the less fortunate in society. It is equally difficult to uphold one's moral standards, when one fills out one's annual income tax report with deduction percentages way above the fifty bracket. Stretching the margins beyond what is legally admissible, is to many no longer an immoral deed. On the contrary, it is often experienced as a sport or a gamble with chances. Most perpetrators of the tax codes are unable to relate their illegal behavior to a moral system, based among others on the value of solidarity. If one still chooses to call such a "tax evasion" immoral, one ought to realize that this immoralism is to an important degree caused by the amoralism of the bureaucratic, almost value-free megastructure, called the welfare state. This is a curious division of the public and the private: the public realm is an amoral, and to many even immoral reality, whereas moral norms and values, are strictly private. We shall return to this point later, when we discuss the ethos of the welfare state.

Legality and Legitimacy

All this brings us to yet another ambiguity inherent to the welfare state and equally hidden behind the seemingly rational façade of rules, regulations, and bureaucratic controls. The welfare state is and always has been a constitutional state in which, as is customary in a democracy, the rule of law reigns. Thus, all the acts by which the state initiates, organizes and finances welfare arrangements in the fields of education, health care, housing, care for the aged, media, labor relations, social security, etc., have to be cast in laws to be passed by parliament. The intensive and extensive welfare state is, as a result, the producer of large amounts of laws. In particular the ministries covering health, welfare and education are true legal mills, producing hundreds of laws and regulations annually.

The legal arrangements concerning social security, for example, are by now in most welfare states of such a complexity that they can only be grasped and understood by a few experts in the field. This massive production of legal arrangements reminds one of inflation. In fact, in a welfare state ministers and ministries are politically evaluated and measured by the amount of laws they send to the parliament for ratification. As was argued before, there are in the context of a comprehensive welfare state scores of pressures from below—from the market and civil society—which call for an *interventionist* state. All the state's actions in response to these demands have to be legalized. Policies are to be forged in laws. This, of course, contributes willy-nilly to the overproduction of policies and laws.

The result of this inflation is, of course, a kind of legalism which exerts scores of formal and abstract pressures on the market and civil society. They are, however, devoid of meaning. As a result, with the expansion of legality there is a proportionate decline of legitimacy. It is not enough to pass laws in a procedurally correct manner. In order to function properly in a democratic society, laws ought to be meaningful, understandable, sensible to the people subjected to them. Just as power functions in a democracy appropriately only, if it is experienced as being legitimate, whereby power is transformed into authority, laws can do their work only, if they constitute a meaningful order—a true *nomos*—borne mentally and emotionally by the members of society.

Legality ought to be transformed into legitimacy. Not sheer legality but legitimacy is the litmus proof of a truly democratic society. The majority of the people, however, does not and cannot believe in the necessity and the justice of all these highly complex and specialized legal arrangements. The result is an initially invisible, but steadily and silently expanding *anomie*. There was in the heyday of the comprehensive welfare state a considerable amount of illegal use of welfare facilities. This was rarely felt as an immoral, unethical, let alone illegal behavior on the part of the perpetrators.

This runs, of course, parallel to the ambiguity of power and authority. Lacking sufficient legitimacy, the welfare state is experienced as, and actually forced to be, a rational megastructure which stands out as a very forceful institution, the direct and coercive power of which is more visible and tangible than its authority. This is, certainly in terms of democracy, one of the weakest spots of a fully developed welfare state. Due to the predominantly economic analyses and interpretations of the welfare state, this point pertaining to its alarmingly weak moral foundations, has often been neglected.

Divergent Interests of Citizens and Professionals

The capitalist mode of production brought about the moral prisoner's dilemma of particular versus general interests. Subjected to competition the actor in the market tries to improve optimally his individual market position and to safeguard his particular interests. Competition keeps him on the ball. Therefore, the choices he makes are truly rational only if he takes into account the interests of competitors also, since their ruin could eventually spell his own decline. The capitalist market would be dead without competition. In other words, monopolies may seem to be advantageous but in the long run they are not. There are large corporations which see to it that their very own subsidiaries engage in mutual competition.

It has been one of the driving forces behind the welfare state to solve this ancient dilemma. In fact, it was the initial dream of its founding fathers that the welfare state, based upon a mixed (partly free, partly planned) economy would constitute the ideal context for a well-understood self-interest. Bismarck, for instance, devised a system of social security, not because he was morally involved with the plight of the working class, but because he wanted to accommodate the interests of the powerful Junker-class and those of the emerging middle-classes. In a sense, his reason of state symbolized the well-understood self-interests of the Junkers and the bourgeoisie.

After World War II it was in particular the socioeconomically expanding and politically rising middle-class that set up the comprehensive welfare state as a megastructure which was supposed to tie the general interests of all members of society, including the working class, to its own bourgeois self-interests. After all the welfare state was initiated by the bourgeoisie, not by the working class. As such it was the product of a well-understood bourgeois self-interest.

However, the welfare state, as it emerged in Western Europe in the 1960s and 1970s, has not been very successful in reconciling these particular and general interests. Sociological research discovered soon that the main beneficiaries of the various welfare services were and remained the representatives of the middle class. Moreover, research demonstrated that particularly in the large cities new forms of poverty and exclusion emerged which apparently could not be avoided, let alone alleviated by the existing arrangements of the welfare state. Its comprehensiveness, in other words, had apparent limits. Certain categories of people (rather than traditional classes), such as the long-term unemployed, the unemployable, single parents, and undocumented migrants, appeared to be particularly vulnerable. It led to various forms of social exclusion, and the steady emergence of a culture of poverty in which alienation and anomie became "normal" pathologies.

In the discussion about the development of social rights it is customary to refer to T.H. Marshall's classic theorem of modern citizenship. As is well known by now, he distinguished in the development of citizenship three ideal-typical stages spread over the eighteenth, nineteenth, and twentieth centuries. The eighteenth century witnessed the rise of *civil rights* such as freedom of speech, the right of property and the right to sign contracts. In the next century citizens acquired *political rights*, among which in particular universal suffrage, anchored in democratic institutions such as the three independent (legislative, executive, and judicial) powers. Citizenship finally reached its conclusion in the twentieth century through the emergence of the *social rights* which contain minimum standards for a civilized, socioeconomically secure life.[8]

Marshall's theorem is often quoted and much debated critically, but the inherent ambiguities and tensions between the three types of rights are customarily overlooked. They are, however, endemic to the extensive and intensive welfare state. In fact, they highlight some of its basic and structural weaknesses. For example, in most European cities *squatting* became in the 1970s a nearly formal institution, condoned by city governments and even legitimated by the courts. The practice of occupying old and deserted buildings kept vacant by owners for speculation purposes, is attacked in court by the owners-speculators with reference to the civil right of ownership. The squatters, however, appeal to the social right of housing, often adding the political opinion that speculators abuse their economic power fostered by the system of capitalism— a system the squatters generally reject.

During the 1980s this ideological standpoint was gradually abandoned. Meanwhile, the institutionalization of the squatting movement gained momentum. Squatters in Amsterdam, for instance, set up an informal housing organization which offers cheap living quarters for the poor to rent. In order to prevent squatting, speculators in turn often recruit students to live in their houses without rent until they decide to sell the property. As was agreed upon beforehand, the students then vacate the premises. Since they have lost political terrain, these squatters have meanwhile branched out. Many of them are active now in the "green movement."

In view of such developments the more general and fundamental question arises whether within the framework of a comprehensive welfare state the social rights have not become parasitic vis-à-vis the earlier rights of citizenship. That is, are the civil and political rights of citizens not in fact threatened by the extensive social rights of the welfare state? This question loses its academic character if one focuses on a single basic feature of the welfare state, namely its inherent *professionalization* and *professionalism*. The care of citizens which in a welfare state is guaranteed by the government, is almost exclusively in the hands of professionals who do their work relatively autonomously in various organizations—schools of primary, secondary, higher and vocational education, hospitals, nursing homes, homes for the elderly, various social welfare institutions, etc.

Organized in their own associations these (predominantly health, education and welfare) professionals often make rather stilted demands, which are presented to the state and to their clients as the necessary standards and preconditions of quality. They develop their own idiosyncratic ideas about their work, and have the ingrained tendency to review their own performances in the light of their own professional ethos and worldview. Clearly, social rights are of great interest to welfare professionals because they stake out the limits of their power and the boundaries of their market. In sum, in view of these developments it remains highly unlikely that the social rights ought to be seen as the finishing touch of democratic citizenship.

Not rarely professionalism goes at the expense of efficiency and effectivity. Although the organizations in which they work are modernized and thus formally bureaucratized, professionals often resemble a quite traditional type of elite. A Dutch observer once spoke aptly of "expertocracy." The concept New Class comes also to mind again in this context. Eliot Freidson spoke of "professional dominance" which subjects clients and patients to dependence and subordinance: they are subjected to the professional care which they have to endure in patience. That is to say, under the regime of these professionals, recipients of care and welfare are in danger of ending up in tutelage, thereby losing essential components of their citizenship. Professional dominance, Freidson argued, has probably advanced most rapidly and radically in the medical sector of the welfare state.[9] Maybe Ivan Illich forced the issue somewhat when he claimed that modern professions create the very opposite of what they are supposed to bring forth. Take this with a grain of salt perhaps, but he may not be totally wrong in claiming that the different professions of the health, education and welfare sectors foster illness, disability, and illiteracy instead of curing them. He called them consequently "disabling professions."[10]

Naturally, *knowledge* and *information* occupy a crucial position in this welfare state professionalism and in the ensuing decline of the essential components of citizenship. Confronted with the expertise of the professional, the client-citizen should command over a minimum of knowledge and information, if he is to maintain some degree of autonomy and self-determination vis-à-vis the professional dominance of the providers of care. This is, as Freidson demonstrated, a notorious problem in the medical field in which professional knowledge is extremely advanced and complicated, but deals simultaneously with our directly experienced reality: our own body. Through education and in particular through the popularization of basic medical knowledge in periodicals and television programs, ordinary people are no longer as naive as former generations. A Dutch sociologist even claimed that one could speak of a "proto-professionalization" of laymen.[11] However, much of this knowledge is ephemeral, deficient, and couched in emotions and irrationalities. It often drifts off into paramedical theories and therapies which, of course, decidedly affect the professional dominance of the medical establishment. Whether these paramedical theories and therapies also fortify laymen's autonomy and freedom, is to be doubted. They often keep people under the irrational tutelage of a magical spell.

Moreover, in order to participate in society fully and have a voice as democratic citizens the welfare state and its social rights require a considerable degree of *legal knowledge*. Research has established that in particular those who need the provisions of the welfare state most, are often unaware of their social rights and lack the knowledge and dexterity to receive what they are entitled to. On the whole, it is representatives of the middle class that manage to benefit most from welfare state provisions and subsidies. Next to legal knowledge a considerable degree of *social knowledge* of institutions and organizations is required in order to find one's way through the rules and regulations, offices and authorities of the welfare state. Both types of knowledge are usually hard to acquire with the result that democratic participation remains faulty. Here again we witness the tragic nature of the welfare state: the more it expands its reach and intensifies its program, the less it is able to realize its ultimate aim—the establishment of a socially just and secure society.

Knowledge can be defined as the ability to order pieces of information into a meaningful whole. Through knowledge the world is viewed and experienced as a relatively coherent and understandable order in which and from which one can live and work. *Information* is therefore the precondition of knowledge, since it contains its constituent components, its building blocks. If one would accept Marshall's three stages of citizenship, one could distinguish a fourth right of citizenship: the right of information.[12] Legal-advice centers and street-level bureaucracies have tried to do justice to the need for information and advice in a complex welfare state. Here too, however, professionalization and bureaucratization, and the endemic call for state subsidies on the part of the involved professionals and bureaucrats, have contributed to the absorption of these institutions into the megastructures of the welfare state.

It was said time and again in the previous discussion: morality occupies a crucial place in the welfare state. It was not exclusively Bismarckian reasons of state that have led to its emergence. The values of liberty, equality, and solidarity, and their related norms have initially inspired those who put up a political fight for its erection. However, this fact was, as we saw, gradually obfuscated while the welfare state expanded into a rather technocratic and bureaucratic megastructure. As a result, the main socio-scientific debates on and scientific investigations of the welfare state failed to acknowledge this moral dimension. We must now focus on it specifically.

Notes

1. H. J. Heering, *Tragiek van Aeschylus tot Sartre* (Tragedy from Aeschylus to Sartre), (The Hague: L.J.C. Boucher, 1961), p. 18f.
2. G. Myrdal, *Beyond the Welfare State: Economic Planning in the Welfare State and its International Implications* (London: Duckworth, 1960), in particular pp. 69–74.
3. For the concept of social capital see James S. Coleman, "Social Capital in the Creation of Human Capital," *American Journal of Sociology* (1988), vol. 94, pp. 95-120. On trust as part of social capital see Francis Fukuyama, *Trust: The Social Virtues and the Creation of Prosperity*, (New York: The Free Press, 1995).
4. See Peter L. Berger and Richard J. Neuhaus, *To Empower People: From State to Civil Society*, new edition introduced and edited by Michael Novak (Washington, DC: The AEI Press [1976]1996).
5. See in particular Robert D. Putnam, "Bowling Alone," *Journal of Democracy* (1995), vol. 6, pp. 65–78.

6. See in particular the report of the working group on equality set up by the Swedish Social Democratic Party: Alva Myrdal, *Equality*, an abridged version translated by Roger Lind (Stockholm: Prisma, 1971). Social-democratic egalitarianism led at times to remarkable statements. Olaf Palme once said in a speech: "Our chief foe is not the reactionary bourgeois politician but an obstinate reality." The speech was entitled "Policy for the '70s" and published by the Social Democratic Party of Sweden in a special edition in 1970.

7. Daniel Bell, *The End of Ideology: On the Exhaustion of Political Ideas in the Fifties* (New York: Collier Books, 1961). Francis Fukuyama, *The End of History and the Last Man* (New York: The Free Press, 1992). Herbert Marcuse who was more a romantic than a Marxist philosopher, came closer to the truth than either Bell or Fukuyama, when he accused the welfare state of absorbing and neutralizing all critical initiatives. He dubbed this "repressive tolerance." See his at the time much applauded yet little understood *One-Dimensional Man: Studies in the Ideology of Advanced Industrial Society*, (Boston: Beacon Press [1964] 1968).

8. T. H. Marshall, *Class, Citizenship and Social Development* (Chicago: The University of Chicago Press, 1964), 78-91.

9. Eliot Freidson, *Professional Dominance: The Social Structure of Medical Care* (New York: Atherton Ptress, 1970); *Profession of Medicine. A Study of the Sociology of Applied Knowledge* (New York: Dodd, Mead and Company, [1970] 1973).

10. Ivan Illich et al., *Disabling Professions* (New York: Marion Boyars, [1977]1992), in particular pp. 11–40.

11. Abram de Swaan, *The Management of Normality: Critical Essays in Health and Welfare* (New York: Routledge, 1990), p. 14 and passim.

12. National Consumer Council, *The Fourth Right of Citizenship* (London: Macmillan Co. for the NCC, 1977).

3

The Ethos of the Welfare State

Anecdotes That Tell a Story

On 25 January 1980 a Dutch newspaper reported a remarkable event in a Dutch court.[1] A young German man was tried for a theft he committed immediately upon leaving jail where he had been confined for an earlier infraction of the law. The judge imposed six months confinement for this case of recidivism. Much to his amazement the young man implored him to impose nine months instead of six! His attorney explained why (I quote the newspaper): "This is the first time that I've done this, your honor, but I plea emphatically for a sentence of at least nine months. If we add the five months which are impending since my client violated his probation, we will reach the time needed for him to complete his much-coveted diploma in industrial woodcraft." Asked to explain this request further, it turned out that the young man had enrolled in an apprentice woodcraft course during his first jail sentence, but was released before he could complete the course and acquire the diploma. Since there was no chance he would be able to finish this education in Germany without tuition, he had willfully burglarized a private home again and made sure he would be arrested. The remarkable fact is that in this case the welfare state which, of course, also tends to the well-being of jail inmates, incited criminal behavior.

It was July 1996. Dutch television reported that the national government considered to terminating the financing of free methadone for drug addicts. The government felt that the cities should pay for it in the future. An urban drug addict appeared on the television screen and calmly explained that if the state or the city would no longer provide him with free methadone, he would have to burglarize in order to obtain the needed means to purchase it. He added that he might also suffer a relapse and start taking heroin again, which would be disastrous for both his family and for society at large. He could next be seen playing tenderly with his young daughter, a plastic cup, symbol of methadone distribution, in one hand. Obviously, the man had learned his welfare state lesson well.

There are scores of similar anecdotes. They are, of course, not fit to be used in a systematic treatise as they run the risk of being dismissed by welfare professionals, welfare state bureaucrats, and social scientists as isolated incidents. However, if sociologists are want to look beyond their theoretical models and statistical tables, they should in a more anthropological vein also take notice of everyday life stories and experiences. If these anecdotes don't scientifically prove, in a strict and neo-positivistic sense, anything they may still reveal a lot about the everyday feelings of ordinary people. And, as in the case of the above anecdotes, they may also sensitize people to the moral state of affairs, which usually remains hidden behind the theoretical models and statistical tables of "true" social science.

In any case, these anecdotes tell a story about the moral foundations, or ethos, of the welfare state. Let us now reflect upon this ethos in a more systematic manner.

Worldview, Ethos, and Welfare State

It has been observed that the welfare state is not founded upon an explicit ideology or worldview like nation-states based upon Marxism, Zionism, or Islam.[2] This is certainly true of the comprehensive welfare state which developed into a rather technocratic and bureaucratic system of redistribution. After all, the intensive and extensive welfare state is a giant megastructure which lacks the legitimacy that social systems need for their long-term survival.

However, we saw before that the project of a welfare state was initially founded upon a determinable set of values. In fact, historically the idea of a welfare state was the late fruit of the Enlightenment and the French Revolution, tying together three basic values and worldviews: liberty, equality, and solidarity. Liberty as individual freedom and as freedom of the market is, of course, the main value of liberalism, while equality as an egalitarian principle has always been the dominant value of socialism. Although the latter would embrace it in its own particular way, namely as class consciousness within the context of a fundamental class conflict, solidarity has been the dominant value of conservatism as it can exist and prosper only in the context of strong, corporatist institutions and communities. Christian democracy in particular has always emphasized solidarity which is seen as the collectivist and moral foundation of a pervasive consensus.

These contradictory worldviews relate to contradictory social policies: liberalism focuses primarily on the free market, socialism on the interventionist state, and conservatism on a strong civil society of traditional, corporatist institutions. So, even if one adjudicates a worldview to it, the welfare state is and always will be an ideologically divided house.

Harold Wilensky has emphasized the technocratic, amoral nature of the welfare state. This is certainly correct as far as the comprehensive welfare states of Western Europe are concerned. However, his reconstruction of the proper origins of the welfare state is rather ahistorical, as he disregards its typically European Enlightenment origins and the basic, contradictory values of the French Revolution. He claims instead that any society that begins to industrialize and develop will be exposed automatically to rather similar economic, technological, and above all demographic developments and demands. His arguments deserve closer attention.

Demography in particular, Wilensky argues, will cause the emergence of primary welfare state services. For instance, industrialization and the remarkable evolution of medical science and medical cure and care will foster the greying of society. This greying cannot be dealt with adequately in the traditional manner, namely by the family. Statutory arrangements for the care of the aged under the aegis of a centralized government are inevitably needed. Indeed, after World War II providing social security for the elderly in society spurred the very start of most welfare states.

Needless to add that this demographic factor is reinforced in the case of a "baby boom" as the one of 1945–55. When this demographic bulk approaches pensionable age, as will happen in the beginning of the next century, the financing of pensions and the care of the elderly will place great financial strain upon any welfare state system. Some may even cave in under the weight of such a burden. In any case, the demographic factor is of crucial importance, if one reflects upon the origins and the chances of survival of the welfare state.

However, as Durkheim in particular would remark, the welfare state as a social and political system could not exist and function properly without an ethos that somehow produces a measure of coherence and integration. Every state and society needs some fundamental moral norms and values which inspire people and bind them, their organizations, and their institutions together, however vague, minimalistic, pluralistic and prereflective these norms and values may be.

In other words, we must ask the Durkheimean question, what is the ethos that keeps a welfare state together? Something moral must keep welfare states together because they are, after all, not the picture of anarchy and chaos. They are in general well ordered, an order which is more than just a technocratic and bureaucratic one. Again, what then is the moral bond—the minimal, socially binding *conscience collective* (Durkheim) that keeps welfare states together?

As could be observed in Sweden and the Netherlands prior to the 1990s, there was, apart from special occasions such as international soccer competitions, no collective sense of solidarity, no strong patriotism let alone nationalism. These countries were also prime examples of fully developed, comprehensive welfare states which were certainly not plagued by anarchy and disorder. What kept them together? Was it sheer bureaucracy, or was there beyond the bureaucratic order some sort of cultural and symbolic order which perhaps did not truly inspire people but yet somehow kept them together emotionally?

This symbolic order, this moral ethos, could not have been an inherent part of the comprehensive welfare state itself. As we just saw, its historical values (liberty, equality, and solidarity) were too contradictory and too vague to inspire people and emotionally bind them together. In this sense Wilensky was right when he viewed the welfare state as an amoral, technocratic megastructure that emerges automatically when a society begins to industrialize and develop. But he also argued that there are cultural conditions that foster, and others that hamper, the development of a welfare state. Some welfare states remained sober and limited in scope, others grew into comprehensive megastructures. Here the cultural factor, Wilensky argues, is a crucial one.

In this chapter I shall argue that a historically developed worldview and ethos can be adverse to and thus hamper the qualitative and quantitative expansion of the welfare state, just as in Weber's view, the Confucian worldview and ethos blocked the development of capitalism and rational-legal bureaucracy in Ancient China, despite the fact that the major material and immaterial conditions for the rise of high capitalism and formal bureaucracy were fully present. Likewise, the worldview and ethos of the "American Creed" (Myrdal) and the closely related prominence of intermediary, decentralized structures (cf. the voluntary associations) stood, in the case of the United States, in opposition to the rise of the comprehensive welfare state on the scale of, say, Sweden or the Netherlands. Despite the cultural, political, and societal idiosyncracies of modern Japan, the same holds true, as we shall see presently, for the worldview and ethos called *Iemoto*.

Before we continue this line of argument, we ought to clarify some basic concepts, in particular *worldview* and *ethos*. *Worldview* is defined here (after Clifford Geertz) as a cognitive conglomerate of opinions and theories about an "assumed structure of reality."[3] Thus, a worldview which, prior to modernization, was mainly religious and magical, and in modernity is predominantly scientific and technological, consists of more or less systematic ideas about an allegedly structured order in nature, history, and society. It is in a fully modernized society a rationalist worldview inspired by the various sciences, acquiring at times the features of a secularized religion. In that case we speak of *scientism*.

Ethos is closely related to this. It tells people how to behave in accordance with the worldview, what kind of normative and esthetic lifestyles one ought to develop and adhere to. It tells people how reality is to be experienced emotionally. An ethos, Geertz wrote aptly, contains ideas about an "approved style of life."[4] Usually the concept of ideology is defined as a worldview which propagates and defends specific (group or class) interests. In this chapter I shall for convenience's sake only use the concept of ethos, but it should be understood that it is linked indissolubly to the concepts of worldview and ideology. Because of its ethos, a group acquires its own character and identity in distinction to other groups. William Sumner elegantly defined an ethos as "the sum of the characteristic usages, ideas, standards, and codes by which a group was differentiated and individualized in character from other groups."[5]

Again, is there an ethos of the welfare state? Or better still, since the comprehensive welfare state as a technocratic megastructure does not possess its own distinct ethos, is there an ethos which, as in an elective affinity, fits the welfare state? In order to answer this question satisfactorily, we must first deal with the close relationship between the welfare state and modernity.

The Basic Criteria of Modernity

When a society develops towards an industrial, bureaucratic, fully urbanized society which is dominated in a very rational manner by the sciences and technology, the welfare state will, sooner or later, also emerge. Or, phrased differently, there may be scores of historical and sociocultural differences between specific nations, yet when modernization sets in welfare state arrangements will be put in place. As a result, some sort of convergence between these otherwise varied nations will emerge.

However, as to the welfare state as the main source of convergence, there still will remain considerable differences in intensity and extensiveness. That is, although in all Western, fully modernized nations, welfare state arrangements exist, in some welfare states these arrangements are very extensive and intensive, in others they are lean and mean, sometimes even rudimentary.

As a rule of thumb one can say that radical (intensive and extensive) modernization will lead to a comprehensive (intensive and extensive) welfare state. It may, at first blush, seem odd to claim that the reverse is also true: societies with restricted, if not rudimentarily developed welfare state arrangements, are less radically modernized. Certainly those who view the United States as a leader of modernity, and also realize that the majority of the American states lags behind most Western European nations as to the comprehensiveness of their welfare state arrangements, may question the validity of this thesis. Are American states less modernized than these Western European nations?

The answer: yes, they are, but in a very specific way. Technologically and scientifically they are not. In fact, technologically and scientifically the United States is still far ahead in modernization. But *socioculturally* several states in the United States lag in modernity when compared to Western European societies with comprehensive welfare state arrangements. To the European visitor, daily life in most suburban American communities seems reminiscent of the culture and morality of the 1950s in Europe.

Consequently, when these European societies were forced (to be discussed in the next chapter) to curb their welfare state arrangements, as happened in the 1980s and 1990s; that is, when the waning of the comprehensive welfare state set in, they considerably reduced the range and depth of their sociocultural modernity. As a result, they began to resemble those American states that had rejected the comprehensive welfare state. This is called, understandably but incorrectly, "Americanization."

There are three criteria of modernity which will be used in the ensuing discussion: economic *affluence*, *structural differentiation* (i.e., division of labor, specialization) and *generalization* of values and norms.

They need not be elaborated in great detail here. Affluence is obviously the result of development. Structural differentiation and cultural generalization need a brief explanation.

In social theory, which from its inception in the nineteenth century focused on modernization, the division of labor has been singled out as the most fundamental motor of development. Development and division of labor are endemic to the human race, but it was industrialism that intensified these processes, leading to an increasingly radical specialization of tasks and functions, that is, an increasingly radical structural differentiation. Culturally, as to the values, norms, and meanings which constitute the symbolic order of a society, this differentiation causes pluralism in which there are scores of relatively autonomous subcultures held together by an overarching national culture which remains vague, general, and abstract.

The national welfare state of Sweden, for example, differs from that of the Netherlands in certain structural details. Thus, the Swedes emphasize labor market participation, while the Dutch until the 1980s primarily focused on universalistic social security. Yet apart from these and other differences (language, political history, religion, etc.), the overall national differences are very vague, general and abstract, not in the least because they both share a comprehensive welfare state regime. This, incidentally, may well be one of the reasons for the relative success of the European Union which prior to World War II would have been unthinkable, if only because major nations like Great Britain, Germany, and France had distinct and contrasting cultural identities.

These three criteria of modernity—affluence, structural differentiation, and cultural generalization—are in concrete societies not distributed in an equal manner. A society is highly modernized when it is affluent, structurally differentiated, and culturally generalized. It is also possible to be affluent and structurally differentiated yet at the same time culturally not very much generalized. An American community in the Midwest, for instance, can be affluent and structurally differentiated but culturally under the spell of traditional, bourgeois values and fundamentalist-religious norms. It is also possible that such a community consciously curbs specialization, emphasizes undifferentiated labor, or, as in the case of the Amish and similar religious groups, rejects all modernization, even if this endangers their affluence (which, remarkably, it has not done).

Such pockets of premodernity, incidentally, also exist in a comprehensive and highly modernized welfare state, as in the case of the Netherlands. In the recent past ultra-Calvinist parents, for instance, have refused on religious grounds their children's inoculation. Since the national state is responsible for the health of the nation and should help to prevent epidemics, it could not honor these parents' appeal to their constitutionally grounded freedom of religious conviction. The state by special court orders has temporarily lifted the control of these parents temporarily, and returned the children to their parents' custody again after they had been vaccinated by the proper medical authority. However, this is a rare example of premodernity in an otherwise sociocultuturally radically modernized society.

Given the fact that the comprehensive welfare state is to all intents and purposes a technocratic and amoral system and given the fact that there are three basic criteria of modernity which can prevail in a society in varying degrees of intensity, we might once again ask the question: which type of ethos might have a positive, which one a neutral, and which one a negative elective affinity or fit with the welfare state?

Logically there are three analytic types of ethos—*ideal types*—which entertain (each one in its own way) elective affinities with the technocratic welfare state: *moralism, amoralism,* and *immoralism.* These three types are also tied in three different bonds to the criteria of modernity. Let us discuss these three types of ethos and their respective ties to modernity first, and then go on to see how they relate to the comprehensive welfare state.

The Moralist Ethos

As to the conditions of modernity, the following criteria apply to this type of ethos: there is a relatively high degree of affluence, and the social structures to which this ethos belongs, are differentiated rather strongly. According to these two criteria, the society in which this ethos functions is rather modern. But, for the time being, the degree of cultural generalization remains relatively low. Meanings, values and norms remain traditional, firmly institutionalized, and they are accepted and followed in a naive, taken-for-granted manner. Society is actually not experienced as an abstract megastructure (*Gesellschaft*), but rather as a concrete community (*Gemeinschaft*) which manages to provide a collective meaning of life. This state of affairs which, despite the affluence and the structural differentiation can be called traditional or premodern, is reinforced by the moralistic type of ethos which bears the following features:

- A clearly distinguishable set of values, norms, and meanings is accepted without much relativizing reflection. They are accepted as God-given, or provided by Nature or Reason. Religious or semireligious moralizing is rife;
- The ethos is optimistic and activistic. The world can be improved by joint actions, and reality can be constructed, made according to common plans and designs. Voluntarism is strong and vital;
- A sense of community is essential. Commitment to and involvement in the affairs of the community are expected of the individual who receives a strong sense of collective identity in return. There is in society a taken-for-granted form of mutual trust and loyalty;
- There is a strong belief in authority and in the role of morally strong leaders who function in an enlightened-authoritarian manner. The ethos has paternalistic features;
- Moral egalitarianism rather than political, social or economic equality reigns and applies first and foremost to members of one's own community. People are distinguished in terms of "them" and "us." This egalitarianism is competitive, but the casualties of competition (e.g., the physically and/or mentally handicapped) are the proper target of voluntary or charitable actions;
- The active participation in the community's affairs is nonpartisan, unconnected with political parties or religious sects, and local;
- Private and public spheres are merged in notions of responsibility and representation. Individualism can be strong but the individual is held accountable for public performance and duty. As a result, social control prevails; and,
- Citizens' rights are held in high esteem but narrowly linked with private and public duties, and they are defined in terms of the collectivity.

American society, particularly outside the metropolitan areas and within WASP-communities, comes to mind, as an example of this type of ethos. But, and this may at first come as a shock, one is also reminded of contemporary Iran and its theocratic, Islamist worldview and ethos. Most societies in Western Europe, on the contrary, have ever more strongly alienated themselves from this type of ethos, which had been quite prominent prior to the spectacular rise of the comprehensive welfare state, say roughly before 1960.

The Moralist Ethos can be illustrated easily in terms of the "American Creed," the "Protestant Work Ethic," or for that matter "Fundamentalist Islamism." But it might be interesting and illuminating to focus on contemporary Japan. Here various components of the Moralist Ethos seem to occur in a historically unique, institutional framework which, apart from this ethos, bears the basic features of modernity.

Next to influential kinship relations, a system called *dozoku*, Japanese society is in possession of an organization principle which is prevalent in the world of arts and crafts, and resembles a kinship system. It is called the *iemoto* which is usually written by means of two Chinese characters that mean respectively "household" and "origin." Francis Hsu, whom I quote here, writes: "In essence it is an organization consisting of a master of some art or skill (i.e., pottery making, flower arranging, calligraphy, judo, songs, etc.) and his disciples. The group is called an *iemoto* and the master is the *Iemoto* of his *iemoto*."[6]

The *iemoto*, which occurs in a broad variety in Japanese society, stands between a guild and a school with its particular style and master: "There are not only the well-known schools of flower arrangements, tea ceremony, judo, painting and calligraphy, but there are also schools of dancing, Kabuki, No drama, archery, horsemanship, singing, cloth designing, koto playing, miniature gardening, cooking, the art of manners, incense burning and, of course, the groups of samurai who are not called *iemoto* but who nevertheless were organized on the same principle."[7] The core of the *iemoto* is the teacher-pupil relationship, which is authoritarian and paternalistic in nature. Its members treat one another as the members of a family, but the *iemoto* is not hampered by the immobilizing and restrictive ties of blood relations and geographical location. It even transcends the limitations which most religious bonds impose on human beings.

Hsu claims that the mentality of this institution has permeated Japanese culture, like an ethos that functions in the end also in those sectors of society that are not formally organized strictly according to the *iemoto* principles. It reminds the cultural sociologist of Weber's account of the "Protestant Work Ethic," the influence of which also transcended its proper religious boundaries: "The spirit of *iemoto* prevails among businessmen, industrial workers, teachers, professors and students in modern universities where the *iemoto* does not formally exist. Its spirit is apparent in the all-inducive and nearly unbreakable command-obedience, succor-dependence relationships between the old and the young, the senior and the junior, the superior and the subordinate. It is well known, for example, that there is very little horizontal mobility among professors of different universities, and employees tend to remain for life in the same business firms in which they began their working careers." [8]

Indeed, Hsu sees the spirit of *iemoto* at work far beyond the arts and crafts. Industrial relations, for instance, are based upon the *oyabun-kobun* (parent-child) relationship within the corporative hierarchy and upon the *onjo shugi* (benign treatment of workers) in corporative personnel policies. The industrial corporation is viewed and experienced as a giant community which at times might be criticized and complained about by the employees, but to which they all feel emotionally related as in some fundamental, family-like solidarity. Meanwhile, management takes care of its employees in a paternalistic manner: their social welfare and security are taken care of by the organization rather than by the state. In exchange the corporation can count on the commitment and loyalty of its employees, irrespective of their rank and order.

The Japanese psychiatrist Takeo Doi added an important element to this: the sentiment of dependence, which is represented by the concept of *amae*. The most fundamental example of *amae* is the warm, natural relationship of dependence between a mother and her child. *Tanin*, Doi explains, is the very opposite: it has a ring of cold indifference, as one might experience with strangers and aliens.[9] The Japanese, Doi argues, have a deep yearning for *amae*-relationships in which they can surrender themselves to others, as in emotional dependence. In *amae* the I and the You, but also the subject and the object, merge into an emotional unification that provides the individual with a deep sense of security.

However, this does not amount to a passive, almost mystical unification. On the contrary, Doi argues, *amae* is narrowly linked to a perpetual sense of imperfection, of not being satisfied with one's performance: *ki ga sumanai*.[10] It is the psychological source of Japan's proverbial industriousness: "In Japan, farm, factory, and office workers throw themselves unquestioningly into their work. It is not so much that they are obliged to do so by poverty, but that if they did not do so they would feel *ki ga sumanai*. They give little consideration to the meaning of their work or to what it will achieve for society as a whole, or for themselves, or for their families.... When a particular stage of his work is finished, of course, even he will feel satisfaction and take a break. But since there is always more work waiting, he soon feels *ki ga sumanai* and start to feel pressed by work again."[11] Naturally, Doi sees a close correspondence with Western Puritanism and its work ethic.[12]

The Amoralist Ethos

As to the conditions of modernity, the following criteria apply to this type of ethos: there is a great deal of material poverty, while the social structure of the society to which this type of ethos fits best, is relatively undifferentiated. In addition, there is also a relatively low degree of cultural generalization, since the values, norms, and meanings remain tightly attached to an established tradition. For the time being religious and/or magical forms of thought have a far greater impact on the consciousness of individuals than scientific and technological ways of thinking and doing things. In short, this is a premodern, traditional society whose dominant characteristic is the fact that its population is subjected to an ongoing struggle for a minimal material level of existence. The ethos appropriate to this kind of society has the following features:

- Pessimism, fatalism, and lethargy are induced by natural disasters, corrupt local elites, and in some instances multinational corporations;
- Communal organization for better life conditions finds little support. People tend to retreat into "amoral familism";[13]
- Individuals who do take initiatives are distrusted as it is assumed they are motivated by personal gains. Distrust reigns in general;
- People acquiesce in the existing structures of power and authority; these structures often establish and maintain order through intimidation and violence as in the case of the mafia in Sicily;[14]
- Equality is an unknown value, while political mobilization against gross inequalities is generally met with distrust and lethargy;
- A public and representative spirit is absent and public office is accepted in a conventional manner within the existing structures of power and authority; as a result there is no firm link between rights and duties; and,
- Informal social control is, outside the above mentioned intimidation and violence, weak and the sources of personal failure are sought in God, the gods, nature, or fate.

"People living on the very edge of subsistence," the British historian Geoffrey Barraclough wrote, "have no time for intellectual pursuits and precious little interest in morality."[15] Poverty, misery, *tristeza*, distrust, and lack of mutual loyalty typify this kind of existence. This is not immoralism but rather amoralism. That is, one can actually not afford the luxury of moralism, let alone of immoralism. In fact, one is doomed to stagnate culturally and emotionally. One lives from day to day, trying to survive. In Durkheimean terms, *anomie*—a deep-seated sense of meaninglessness and purposelessness—reigns in this type of society.

If one searches for illustrations of this type of ethos, one can, of course, look to many so-called Third World countries. Within the Western hemisphere, Amoralism has been quite prevalent in the urban working class of the nineteenth century. Naturally the modern brand of the culture of poverty, that is, "New Poverty," is also conducive to the amoralist type of ethos. Edward Banfield's study of peasants in southern Italy, or Anton Blok's work on Sicily also provide telling illustrations of amoralism.

Needless to add that the Amoralist Ethos precludes the emergence of a civil society which, of course, stands in need of mutual trust and loyalty, of citizens' initiatives in the context of vital voluntary associations. It also is at odds with a vital market which functions well only if private interests are tied to collective interests within the context of free competition.

The Immoralist Ethos

The following criteria indicate the level of modernization of the social conditions of this ethos type: there is a relatively high degree of affluence, the social structures are strongly differentiated and there is, on top of a strong cultural pluralism, a rather high level of generalization of values, norms, and meanings. Thus, this ethos flourishes in a prosperous, very modern and generally abstract society. Meanings, values, norms and motives are no longer attached clearly and unequivocally to tradition and traditional institutions, such as the church, the nation-state, and the family, but have become socially free-floating, that is, noncommittal. They are easily exchangeable, permanently reflected upon and discussed, and emotionally consumed in a subjectivist manner.

There is a remarkable paradox at work here. Human action is strongly specialized and is couched in many formal (bureaucratic) structures in which functions and procedures have lost their means-to-an-end character, gradually superseding meanings and cultural substances. This led to the following paradox, which Mannheim observed some forty years ago: while modern life has become increasingly abstract and rational, modern human beings have become increasingly emotional and irrational. In Mannheimean and Weberean terms: the increase of functional rationality occurred in modernization at the expense of substantial rationality.

The Immoralist Ethos, then, bears the following characteristics:

- Traditional values and norms are permanently open to question, if not rejected. They are seen as intrinsically relative and socioeconomically conditioned;
- Emphasis is placed upon personality, spontaneity, freedom, experience, and

emotion, rather than on hard work, production, and a job. Naturally the link between rights and duties is weak, if not absent. Trust and loyalty are generally treated with suspicion as they are viewed as rather old-fashioned values that hamper individual experience and self-expression;

- Experiences are consumed. Not only goods and services, but feelings, ideas and scores of happenings, including revolutions and rebellions, are consumed until found unsatisfying and boring;

- Hard work, if at all present, is accepted by the workaholic as an experience, a commodity to be consumed, and a road to self-expression. Its material yields—high salaries—are consumed in a postmaterialist fashion. Eastern religions, usually solidly "Westernized," and esoteric philosophies (New Age, astrology) are embraced in the hours of leisure;

- Motives and results of human actions are separated, while style supersedes content. In the sense that cultural style supersedes substantive and innovative creativity, we may speak of decadence;[16]

- The immoralist has no clear understanding of community but rather speaks of "society," "social structure" or "state" as abstract sources of personal alienation. If there is a quest for community, it is a search for an emotionally gratifying *Gemeinschaft*. The ethic of ultimate ends (Weber: *Gesinnungsethik*) supersedes the ethic of responsibility (Weber: *Verantwortungsethik*);

- Involvement, if at all existent, is an emotional and always temporary *engagement*. It is not a deeply felt commitment to a cause. It is easy to get immoralists on the street for a demonstration because it might be fun to do. It is hard to organize them for a longer period of time, let alone to bind them to a party and to party control;

- Authority, usually defined as top-down power, is rated low, equality, usually defined as an equality of results rather than of opportunities, is rated high;

- Since unequal results are even in the most prosperous of societies unavoidable, dissatisfaction and resentment will always be present. Resentment is reinforced by incessantly rising expectations. Since there are for this resentment not sufficient miseries to focus on in the prosperous societies of the West, it will be focused on what the German sociologist Helmuth Schelsky has called "borrowed misery."[17] The media display starving children in the Third World, and victims of wars and natural disasters in remote parts of the globe. Emotional commitment is then expressed by donation of a gift via a bank account; and,

- The notion of a public realm for which the individual bears responsibility is weakly developed, if at all present. The immoralist sees the "society," the "state," the "bureaucracy" as the realms of inauthenticity and alienation. A pervasive and rather invisible antiinstitutional mood permeates this ethos.

Before we discuss a few examples of this type of ethos, it should be said explicitly that the concepts of moralism and immoralism are used here in a technical-theoretical sense, that is, without value-judgments. Both words have, of course, negative connotations in every day parlance: being called a moralist or an immoralist is usually not meant as a compliment. In the present discussion these concepts are analytical ideal-types which overemphasize certain dimensions of reality at the expense of others, and this is done for heuristic purposes. Only a little introspection and self-knowledge will teach most of us that we have at times a good share of the one type of ethos and at other times feel attracted by the other. It is sociologically very difficult to separate contemporary mankind into "moralists" and "immoralists." The two ideal-types are dimensions, or forces which struggle, as it were, for prominence. The relative prominence of the forces depend, it is being argued here, on intricate elective affinities with socioeconomic and cultural circumstances.

As to amoralism, even when living under affluent conditions this type of ethos can get hold of us. In fact, there are two realms in modern life which profess amoralism, although this is contested: bureaucracy and science. The bureaucrat is expected to treat citizens in a nonpartisan manner and *sine ira ac studio*, whereas the scientist conducts research and interprets reality as much as possible without value-judgments. We all know the limits of this amoralist "objectivity," thus we do not need to discuss them further. Anyhow, in most Western societies the other two ethos types are of more importance. We primarily focus on them in this chapter.

If we then look for examples of the Immoralist Ethos, we can find them in the nineteenth century among the artistic romanticists and philosophical irrationalists. Oscar Wilde and Friedrich Nietzsche come to mind: each in their own idiosyncratic way put up a fight against the Moralist Ethos of their days. They both exemplified and promoted this type of ethos, far beyond their own lifetime. In present-day culture many so-called postmodernists who emphasize irony, contingency and esthetic irrationalism, as successors of and antidotes to Enlightenment rationalism, bear testimony to the Immoralist Ethos, as is clearly demonstrated by the dictum that "anything goes."[18] There are, according to the postmodernists, as far as morality is concerned no legitimate and valid borders and barriers anymore dictated in a top-down manner, gyrating around a single, traditional center. Now, after God and the related religious virtues had been declared dead, the end of the Human Subject, its Ratio and their bourgeois values and norms is announced— not solemnly, of course, but with an ironic grin. This kind of ethos, I shall now argue, fits the comprehensive welfare state best, much better than the moralist type of ethos, let alone the amoralist type.

The Welfare State and the Three Types of Ethos

The relationship between the welfare state and the *Moralist Ethos* is quite antagonistic. It is, to begin with, hard for an extensive and intensive welfare state to get a firm hold on the community towards which this type of ethos is so strongly oriented. This community will not be subsidized by a state and resists legal and bureaucratic rules and regulations. Voluntary associations, so typical of such a community, can and are frequently subsidized, if alone by means of tax exemptions. Yet, they are in general averse and even suspicious of state largesse, since the strings of rules and controls are, of course, attached to it. After all, who pays the piper chooses the tune. Moreover, and this is a much graver objection, state subsidies might in the end threaten the commitment and initiatives of the volunteers on whose dedication voluntary associations depend. Before one knows it, amateurish voluntarism is superseded by rationalized professionalism. Moreover, fund-raising is an important means to secure the commitment and loyalty of volunteers, and it is always narrowly linked to various charitable activities. This is, of course, contrary to the welfare state which dispenses its services and subsidies, including the transfer of income, in a bureaucratic manner.

It is equally hard for the welfare state to get hold of the endemic apolitical individualism of this ethos. Collective spending for the benefit of the welfare package, for instance, is generally abhorred by the true adherents of the Moralist Ethos, not in the least because it is done in such an abstract manner. After a fund-raising project or charitable event, members of a voluntary organization are able to present the collected money personally to the recipients of their benefaction, whereas the recipients of welfare state largesse remain anonymous numbers in a bureaucratic system. They receive their checks by mail, while the financial resources of the system have been collected through a complex and abstract tax and excise system.

Citizens, we argued before, ought to believe that the usually sharply progressive, direct and indirect taxes are the expression of their solidarity with the less fortunate in society, but this rather moralistic argument is in the case of a truly comprehensive welfare state, of course, not very convincing. The welfare package does not require any commitment or initiative on the part of anybody, nor can any moral energy be invested into it. If it comes to it, nobody bears responsibility, nobody is accountable, nobody needs to show loyalty, let alone gratitude, and nobody has to make real, individualized commitments. Naturally, the Moralist Ethos stands square to all this, as the notions of individual responsibility and accountability, individual freedom and initiative are its very essence and core. In short, there is between the welfare state and this type of ethos a negative elective affinity.

If the welfare state and the society regulated by it do not fit this type of ethos, which type of state and society does? The answer is: traditional capitalism and liberalism with their strong emphasis upon "free enterprise" and a solid "work ethic." It is a socioeconomic and political system with but a minimum of state intervention, a maximum of decentralization and privatization, the principle of ownership of the means of production by the owners of capital (stock holders), the principle of competition in a free market, and so forth. Above all, it is the maintenance of social order by means of voluntary associations and similar intermediary structures in a vital civil society.

The relationship between the welfare state and the *Amoralist Ethos* is quite different. To begin with, as a predominantly technocratic structure without a clear worldview and ethos of its own, the welfare state, in particular the comprehensive welfare state, bears amoral features. The Amoralist Ethos, therefore, does not stand square to the welfare state, and the welfare state in its turn can in principle master the amoralist type of ethos. It is actually a relationship based upon mutual indifference, as they do not attract, nor reject each other. If, for some reason, one decides to disregard the lethargy of this ethos and to erect a welfare state, if necessary by force, one could do so relatively easily, since, unlike the Moralist Ethos, the Amoralist Ethos would not actively resist such modernization. As is actually the case in many developing countries, a radical, socialist model of the welfare state has been imposed on an impoverished society with a disoriented, postcolonial culture couched in anomie and amoralism. However, all this offers fertile ground for unbridled corruption since a vital civil society, and the stamina and strength to criticize and bridle the aspirations of local elites are absent. Such corruption makes a mockery of the original intentions of any welfare state, namely to bring about social justice and social security for all people concerned.

If the Moralist Ethos is opposed and the amoralist ethos indifferent to the welfare state, the *Immoralist Ethos* entertains a close, if not warm relationship with it. In fact, there is a strong mutual attraction, a true positive elective affinity comparable to the one Weber discovered between the Protestant Work Ethic and the Spirit of Capitalism. The welfare state can easily control immoralist individuals, it does in fact stimulate and strengthen this type of ethos, whereas conversely the immoralist ethos sustains and reinforces the technocratic character of the welfare state and its in-built lack of moral principles. The main dimensions of this curious elective affinity deserve further analysis.

A crucial component of this mutual affinity is the emphasis on consumption in the Immoralist Ethos. In fact, one could speak of a true consumption ethic. It is an attitude and mentality that perfectly fit the various programs and activities of the comprehensive welfare state, whereas the other way around the inherent irrationalism of the consumption ethic can easily be manipulated by it. As we have seen, the intensive and extensive welfare state consists of countless officials and professionals who produce and administer a broad scale of statutory services far beyond strict welfare and social security. Naturally, it is in their best interest to have more clients who are eager to call for these provisions and who eagerly prepared to consume them. It is simply a matter of supply and demand, and it stands to reason that here too the supply has a strong tendency to trigger the demand. Unlike the Moralist and Amoralist Ethos, the Immoralist Ethos with its endemic consumption ethic produces clients who are eager to consume abundantly. Not only material and immaterial goods, such as food, clothes, furniture, and ideas, emotions and experiences, but also—and in a comprehensive welfare state above all—welfare services like those of education, housing, health, and old age care are in great demand. In fact, the law of rising expectations is set to work under the regime of an Immoralist Ethos which places a larger premium on consumption than on production. This has gradually changed the original nature of the welfare state: it does no longer guarantee *minimal* standards of welfare and well-being, but is counted on as the prime provider of a *maximum* of welfare, security, well-being, and even happiness. Needless to add, such a goal can never materialize. Oceanic expectations, we all know, cause Durkheimean anomie.

Under the pressure of these rising expectations the intensive and extensive welfare state developed into a Land of Cockaigne for which only the sky seemed to be the limit. These expectations, it should be again noted, were rising in the minds and souls of people who needed the often abundant subsidies of the welfare state least: the relatively well-to-do middle classes. And those who needed its services most, often were unable to acquire them for lack of basic information and bureaucratic skills. Meanwhile, the public deficit grew steadily and seemingly incessantly, while due to rising expectations, the citizens of the growing comprehensive welfare state remained dissatisfied with its performances. This is the tragic situation discussed before: while the welfare state intensified and expanded, it failed to realize its proper goals and it lost more and more sympathy and emotional support among the clients it intended to serve abundantly. The more it expanded, the more it suffered a loss of legitimacy.

In a sense this course of events is illustrated by the dialectical change of the so-called principle of *subsidiarity*. It meant originally that sociopolitical regulations and interventions by the state were needed only as long as effective initiatives could not be expected from lower authorities and from the self-regulating organizations of citizens in civil society. They were, however, to be terminated when citizens could effectively take care of their own affairs. In a full-fledged welfare state this principle is actually reversed, since private initiative, if it does occur at all, tends to channel its activities towards the providing state, its administrative officials, and its care professionals at the first opportunity. This dialectical reversal of subsidiarity usually begins with the requisition of state subsidies, and is next consolidated by welfare professionals whose interests are served best by the interventionist welfare state. Particularly within the quaternary sector, nongovernmental and nonstatutory initiatives and activities are often felt to be illegitimate.

During the 1970s I met a young journalist who together with some friends had set up a local newspaper, dealing primarily with the daily events of this provincial town. The paper was produced by a small staff and financed with the revenue from advertisements. The actions and inactions of the politicians and officials at city hall were followed critically but fairly. Not before long, she was summoned to city hall by one of the officials. City hall had taken notice, he told her, of this praiseworthy initiative, and discovered that the editors had failed to requisition the available statutory subsidies. He inquired when the appropriate request would be made, and had the forms waiting in front of him on his desk. When she told him that her paper did not need such subsidies and in fact was strongly opposed to them, as it wanted to maintain its editorial independence, his reaction was one of amazement and disbelief. The enterprising lady and her friends exhibited an ethos that obviously was very much at odds with the expectations and requirements of the official who represented so dutifully and with the best intentions his welfare state and its appropriate ethos.

Meanwhile, despite much dissatisfaction and regular complaints about alleged alienation incurred by an unresponsive state and its bureaucracy, the Immoralist Ethos does in fact sustain and promote the functioning of the comprehensive welfare state. To begin with, its endemic uncommittedness fortifies the welfare state's technocracy, whereas its unremitted demands and expectations stimulate its supply of increasing statutory services. Its rather emotional ethic of ultimate ends also agrees with the comprehensive welfare state simply because it transcends its down-to-earth, amoral technocracy. An ethic of responsibility would be far more inimical to the welfare state.

In addition, the previously mentioned antiinstitutional mood of the Immoralist Ethos—the emotional protest against traditional institutions like the church, the state, and the family—reinforces the welfare state's apparatus and broadens its range of operations. In fact, it weakens the position of civil society and fosters the centralized powers of the state, causing the rise of "etatism," or "statism" without totalitarian intentions. Thus, the gradual decline of the extended family, for example, fostered bureaucratic state control over the nuclear family (child allowances, study grants, compulsory primary and secondary education, etc.). In fact, this institution is now under the firm control of civil servants and state-supported professionals like teachers, social workers, child psychologists, pediatricians, and so forth.

All this leads to an interesting conclusion. The ethos of immoralism is, of course, not the product of the welfare state as there are welfare states in which this type of ethos is not prevalent at all. Moreover, immoralism as worldview and ethos occurred in Western civilization long before the welfare state emerged. Nietzsche, Schopenhauer, Wilde, and nineteenth-century Romanticism in general clearly testified to that fact. Conversely, the welfare state in its turn cannot be viewed as the product of the Immoralist Ethos, as it must be seen primarily as the product of technocratic, material and demographic developments. Thus, both have their own history and their own development. However, they coalesced in Western Europe after World War II and stimulated one another as in a remarkable elective affinity. It is this elective affinity that explains the comprehensiveness of Western European welfare states.

This conclusion then raises the question of why the Immoralist Ethos and its elective affinity with the welfare state became so prominent in Western Europe and not in the United States. The answer has to be sought, in my view, in the relatively long European history of *vertical* social structures and centralized political systems, which was discussed in the previous chapter. We must return to this point once more.

Why was it that the Moralist Ethos in America outside of the metropolitan areas has been more resistant to immoralism than has been the case in most Western European societies? How has it been possible that, despite a fundamental modernization, the ethos of moralism continued to function as a countervailing force and buffer against the rise of a fully fledged, comprehensive welfare state? As has been observed since Tocqueville and Weber, the most important factor has been a predominantly horizontal social structure combined with America's predominantly decentralized political system. The tenacious political history of feudalism and absolutism in Europe and its equally tenacious vertical religious structures (the state-churches of traditional Germany, Scandinavia, Great Britain, and the system of pillarization in the Netherlands) functioned historically as smooth conductors of state interventionism, and of welfare statism. In fact, due to the cultural generalization and the concomitant process of secularization, these vertical structures lost their ideological stamina and in a sense ran empty. That facilitated their conductor functions vis-à-vis the increasingly comprehensive welfare state.

America, in contrast, has always maintained the predominantly horizontal social and political structures which it erected right from the outset in an intentional deviation from the verticalism it had left behind in Europe. This horizontalism is very conducive to a Moralist Ethos and inimical to a comprehensive welfare state. Horizontalism versus verticalism—that has been and still is indeed the essential difference between America and Europe—a historical and fateful difference which strongly influenced the distinct courses their modernization and their welfare states have taken.[19]

Ethos and the Reconstruction of the Welfare State

However, the comprehensive welfare state in Western Europe is waning! In fact, it had run its course in most Western European countries at the end of the 1970s and in the beginning of the 1980s. We have witnessed in the past ten or fifteen years not so much the end of the welfare state as such, but the fundamental and often even radical *transformation* of the *comprehensive* welfare state. Its deficits began to reach an alarming level, its rules and regulations stifled the market, its subsidies ruined competition, its officials and service professionals lamed civil society. The reduction and fundamental transformation of the comprehensive welfare state was more than an economic and political task, for which it was predominantly held in the 1980s. It became ever more apparent that such a transformation presented above all a social, cultural, and particularly moral task as well.

Now, in view of this transformation that began after 1980 and continued into the 1990s, it is of interest to note the fact that the comprehensive welfare state is actually a rather fragile system. It may with all its etatism and interventionism seem to be a robust and even awe-inspiring megastructure, yet not just its economic but also its moral foundations are actually quite weak. In fact, its legitimacy is, as was shown, nearly absent. The ethos that fits its technocratic nature best, is imbued with a lack of loyalty and commitment. When, after the two oil crises of the 1970s, it became apparent that the comprehensive welfare state everyone had grown accustomed to had to be restructured drastically, there were very few people prepared to come to its defense. It is remarkable in the past ten or fifteen years how weak the opposition to the conservative and neo-liberal critics of the welfare state has been. Even most social democrats from whom one would expect a staunch defense of the comprehensive welfare state, joined the call for more market freedom and competition, for decentralization and privatization, for revitalization of civil society. Gone were the Alva Myrdals and the Olof Palmes!

Meanwhile, together with the gradual reduction and decline of the comprehensive welfare state in most Western European societies a commensurate change occurred in the cultural and moral climate. Despite the fact that—mainly among representatives of the New Class of former days—postmodernism kept the immoralist type of ethos alive, one could witness a change of wind in those sectors that really count—the market and civil society at large. In short, the Moralist Ethos was on the rise again. There was first in the 1980s the reassessment of the relevance of a free market, of competition, and of profit making. In fact, there was a new kind of business orientation which even affected the public sector where techniques of modern management and responsible governance were gradually introduced. The work ethic also reemerged.

Needless to say, the Immoralist Ethos could not be of much use in this changing climate. During the 1980s and then especially in the 1990s a reassessment of civil society and its institutions took place. A quest for binding values and norms, borne of trust and loyalty, emerged. There was simultaneously a reassessment of the role of the nuclear family and the school in the transference of values and norms to children. This was translated intellectually into a rethinking of the importance of community, as in *communitarianism*, and of institutions, as in *neo-institutionalism*. From the point of view of the Immoralist Ethos, which even today has not disappeared in toto, all this is frowned upon as neo-conservatism, and as to the reassessment of the market, as neo-liberalism.

In view of the preceding analysis, however, it should rather be seen as the sociological consequence of the end of the comprehensive welfare state. In other words, it is more than a change in ideology and moral climate. It is a structural transformation of a type of society, economy, polity, and culture which we used to call the Welfare State. Maybe we are heading for a time in which this concept will no longer make sense. Is that what we really want to happen? We will return to this question in the final chapter. But first we must discuss in more detail the fundamental transformation of the comprehensive welfare state.

Notes

1. *Nieuwsblad van het Zuiden*, 25 January 1980, p. 7.
2. See in particular Harold Wilensky, *The Welfare State and Equality. Structural and Ideological Roots of Public Expenditures* (Berkeley and Los Angeles: University of California Press, 1975).
3. Clifford Geertz, *The Interpretation of Cultures* (New York: Basic Books, 1973), p. 129.
4. Idem. "A people's ethos is the tone, character, and quality of their life, its moral and aesthetic style and mood; it is the underlying attitude toward themselves and their world that life reflects." Ibid., p. 127.
5. William Graham Sumner, *Folkways* (New York: Mentor Books, [1906]1960), p. 48. See also p. 76.
6. Francis L. K. Hsu, *Iemoto: The Heart of Japan* (New York: John Wiley, 1975), p. ixf. See also Chie Nakane, *Japanese Society* (London: Penguin Books, [1970]1979), p. 60f, 122.
7. Hsu, *Iemoto.*, p. 62.
8. Ibid., p. 151.
9. Takeo Doi, *The Anatomy of Dependence*, translated by J. Bester (Tokyo: Kodansha International, [1971]1986), p. 36f.
10. Ibid., p. 109–13.
11. Ibid. , p. 111.
12. Ibid., p. 112.
13. Edward C. Banfield, *The Moral Basis of a Backward Society* (New York: The Free Press, [1958]1965), pp. 85–104.
14. Anton Blok, *The Mafia of a Sicilian Village, 1860–1960*, (New York: Harper Torchbooks, 1975).
15. Geoffrey Barraclough, *Turning Points in World History* (London: Thames and Hudson, [1977]1979), p. 41.

16. Such an ethos weakens the capacity to ward off external threats and dangers. See Robert M. Adams, *Decadent Societies* (San Francisco: North Point Press, 1983), p. 36: "This indeed is the simplest definition of decadence; it is not failure, misfortune, or weakness, but deliberate neglect of the essentials of self-preservation—incapacity or unwillingness to face a clear and present danger."

17. Helmuth Schelsky, *Der selbständige und der betreute Mensch* (Stuttgart: Seewald Verlag, 1976), p. 22.

18. Naturally Richard Rorty's insightful and readable essays come to mind here: *Contingency, Irony, and Solidarity* (Cambridge: Cambridge University Press, 1989).

19. See my 'Civil Society, Pillarization, and the Welfare State,' in: Robert W. Hefner, *Democratic Civility. The History and Cross-Cultural Possibility of a Modern Political Ideal* (New Brunswick, NJ: Transaction Publishers, 1998), pp. 153–74.

4

The Shaking of the Welfare State

The New Class and the Welfare State

Until the two oil crises of the mid-1970s, the nations of Western Europe enjoyed steady economic growth. Employment was high, prosperity increased annually, and there was an ideological climate which favored a comprehensive welfare state that actively intervened in almost all aspects and corners of the lives of its citizens through subsidies, services, taxes, excises, and infinite streams of policies. In the process the notion of welfare acquired, as we saw, nearly epic proportions. There was cultural and political unrest, particularly at the end of the 1960s and the beginning of the 1970s, expressed in acts of rebellion against the main institutions of traditional authority, primarily the university. At times this unrest grew into fierce political protests, particularly in light of the seemingly never-ending Vietnam War.

Yet in most Western European countries these upheavals were directed primarily against a bygone, rather traditional culture, not against the modern, comprehensive welfare state. By no means did they prevent the further development and expansion of the welfare state. On the contrary, the 1960s were the beginning of its heyday. Not the market, not civil society, but the actively (often hyper-actively) intervening state grew into, and was generally accepted as the focal point of social, cultural, economic, and political gravity.

There were a few Cassandras who had warned prior to 1970 of a situation in which the state was actually overcharged and overexerted—economically, socially, politically and, although this point received much less attention, culturally and morally as well. These warnings were not heeded. But that changed dramatically during the 1970s and 1980s, when it became ever more obvious that the comprehensive, actively intervening welfare state was unsustainable. Many analysts claim today that the two oil crises of the 1970s spelled the beginning of the end of the intensive and extensive welfare state. Although they were, of course, not the only cause, these oil crises did certainly put a halt to the welfare state's steady expansion until that point. They inaugurated, to begin with, the end of a period of full employment, ushering in decades in which unemployment presented one of the major policy problems that the welfare state, initially set up as a guarantee against "idleness," apparently could not solve. In fact, it gradually began to dawn on all concerned that the comprehensive welfare state itself may well be the very source of this tenacious unemployment problem!

Perhaps more disconcerting was the fact that in conjunction with structural unemployment a new kind of poverty began to emerge, particularly in the big cities, amongst special social categories, such as one-parent families, senior citizens with inadequate pensions, and ethnic minorities. The latter were the so-called guest workers and their descendants attracted from Southern Europe, Turkey and Morocco in the 1960s, when there was an urgent shortage of unskilled and low-skilled labor. The New Poverty, as it came to be called, led to social exclusion, and then to an urban culture of poverty from which it was well-nigh impossible to escape. It also proved to be impervious to various welfare programs and simultaneously porous to social vices like drug addiction and crime.

Another trend began to undermine the very foundations of the radical welfare state as it had been set up after the 1950s. Demographic projections indicated a relatively rapid ageing and concurrent degreening of the population. The combination of a decline in fertility (actually below the level of population replacement) and greater longevity put the welfare state under heavy pressures. The OECD forecasted that in 2040 20–25 percent of the population of OECD-countries will be older than sixty-five, and 10–12 percent older than age seventy-five, which is double the percentages of 1986. Since health costs are the highest at the end of a life span, the public health expenditures would increase astronomically in the foreseeable future. The economic pressures on the younger population would multiply when the number of pensioners would increase at the rate projected by the demographers. At the present time, pensions and health care provisions cover the majority of the expenditures of the welfare state. In short, future generations will be burdened, according to these projections, with a very ominous legacy: in many cases a colossal national deficit, and the prospect of a "greying" and "degreening" society with proportional burdens of health care and pension costs.[1]

These and other facts are, of course, crucial for a proper understanding of the major transformations of the Western European welfare states after roughly 1980. Yet, there is a common flaw in most of the predominantly socioeconomic, public-administrative and policy-oriented analyses. They fail to bare the inherent structural weaknesses of the welfare state project. It is as if they view the reductions initiated after roughly 1980, as an externally induced process which overcame the welfare state as a fateful event. Most Western European social scientists, economists, and public policy specialists are at heart proponents of an extensive and intensive, actively intervening welfare state, even though they do realize that the comprehensive welfare state is an impossible dream and even though they do employ the neo-liberal jargon of free enterprise, competition, and privatization.

The advocates of the comprehensive welfare state belong, as we saw before, to the New Class, also called the Knowledge Class—the elite of the postindustrial society. Their ideological sentiments prevented them for a long time from facing the endogenous faults of the comprehensive welfare state, in particular as far as its cultural and moral foundations were concerned.[2] They claimed and professed to be critical theorists but adulated nevertheless for a relatively long time the status quo which the welfare state represented.

There was still another fault in the socio-scientific analyses of the welfare state. Despite much lip service paid to critical, left-of-center theories and theorems, the dominant sociological orientation—whose *Sitz im Leben* was very much the welfare state itself—remained predominantly "functionalist" and "positivist," an orientation which has always been notoriously insensitive to a more historical, cultural, and moral approach. This orientation had much to do with the postwar situation in which all forces in society had to be summoned to rebuild and reconstruct the economy, the infrastructure, the organizations, and institutions of civil society. As to the contribution of the social sciences, it was expected that they too would be applicable, policy oriented, and practically useful. Sociology and psychology in particular were called upon, and often lavishly funded, to contribute to the interventions of the emerging welfare state by means of applied research. Understandably, the welfare state became their vested interest.

However, ideological orientations are flexible. It is remarkable from the point of view of the sociology of knowledge to observe how after 1980 the New Class adjusted itself to the new circumstances, and in fact exhibited itself ever more blatantly as a fierce proponent of the

free market, of a new type of private management and public administration, and of a retreating, decentralizing, and privatizing state. This,
it should be realized, is not a radical shift, an ideological *volte face*, an
essential turnaround of political orientation. On the contrary, as we have
seen, the New Class consisted of "hidden technocrats" who designed,
planned, and maintained the comprehensive welfare state, and often
did so under the guise of a sociopolitical, left-of-center stance. Most of
them, however, have "come out" after 1980, and are now blatantly free-
market, liberalist technocrats who devote their time and energy to the
deconstruction, if not destruction, of the welfare state they supported
and admired so much before 1980. Today, most formerly left-of-center
socialists preach the neo-liberal gospel of the free market. The constant
factor in their worldview is a rather unimaginative, functionalist and
positivist technocracy founded upon the Immoralist Ethos which is now
called "postmodernist."

Meanwhile, the comprehensive welfare state began its transformation in the 1980s. It has been, we can conclude in retrospect, a major
shake-up, but certainly not the end of the welfare state. Ever since this
remarkable decade in which the political map of the world changed
dramatically with the collapse of the Soviet Imperium, there has been a
search for a socioeconomically and culturally as well as morally
sustainable welfare state. It makes sense to survey the most influential
processes which, given the crudely economic necessity to reduce public expenditures, led to a much more restricted, sober, and lean welfare
state. Now verywhere in Western Europe, even in left-of-center governments, there is a call for a return of the state to its core business, for
a strengthening of the organizations and institutions in civil society, for
decentralization, deregulation, and privatization, for a concurrent
revitalization of the market and thus the economy within the context of
an increasingly transnational, global competition.

Towards a European Welfare State?

The welfare state, it should be noted, has always been a project limited by national and geographic borders. The social rights it set out to
fulfill and guarantee were, as T.S. Marshall has argued, the copestone
of citizenship. Strictly taken, only citizens of a particular nation-state
were entitled to statutory services, like social security, education, housing, health care, and care of the elderly. In a sense, the only hard limits
imposed on a national welfare state were its geographical borders. Natu-

rally, the financing of these ever expanding and intensifying public services had to be realized also within the strictures of these geographical borders.

Citizens and national corporations were taxed in order to finance the national welfare state programs. This was, so to say, the lifeline of the comprehensive welfare state, and precisely on this point important changes took place since roughly the 1970s.

National corporations, in particular the large, financially strong multinationals, have become, as it were, "footloose." They began to operate in the 1980s in a global market and thus transcended the borders of their nation of origin. There are scores of financial, above all fiscal advantages attached to this globalization, much to the financial detriment of the national welfare state. Affluent citizens too discovered scores of fiscal escape routes beyond national borders. It is notoriously hard for the tax authorities of a nation-state, to which these legal tax evaders belong in terms of citizenship, to prevent this sizable loss of state income. National borders have become porous, making it quite easy not only for undocumented migrants, notoriously burdensome to national finances, to enter but also for tax-paying citizens and corporations to exit.

Once more, the welfare state was initially meant as a strictly national project for citizens living rightfully within the borders of a national territory. However, since the 1970s this territorial principle has lost much of its significance. Take for example the financial fluctuations since the collapse of the Bretton-Woods system in the beginning of the 1970s. The result has been floating exchange rates and a spectacular increase of speculative transactions in global financial markets. It has been claimed that in this so-called casino-capitalism transaction volumes of one trillion dollars per day take place.[3] Due to the spectacular developments in information technology, information and communication too transcend national borders on a global scale, twenty-four hours a day no less.

Most European nation-states have, of course, voluntarily cooperated in opening, if not even in lifting, their national borders. The close economic cooperation within the European Union (the EU, as the European Community was named at Maastricht in 1992), initiated by the Treaty of Rome in 1957 (Germany, France, Italy, and Benelux, i.e., Belgium, Luxembourg, and the Netherlands), developed gradually into a social, cultural, and above all political cooperation. With the Treaty of Maastricht (1992) the EU opened the road towards a monetary union

(EMU with the introduction of one European currency, the *euro*, at the Amsterdam meeting in 1997), and beyond that even to a possible political union (EPU). There are, of course, still many obstacles ahead, not the least of which are strong national sentiments on the part of those Europeans who want and demand to maintain their own traditional and morally binding sentiments of national identity. This identity, it is argued, is founded on ancient institutions, such as the monarchy, the nation-state, the currency, etc., which embody a coveted national sovereignty. In most European countries, one should not forget, national sovereignty had been violated in the past by various wars. Now its sovereignty should not be swallowed up by an abstract political construction ruled by transnational bureaucrats in the capital of the EU, Brussels. This "euroscepticism," however, is opposed by the notion that precisely this past of internecine European wars demand the close economic, political, and sociocultural cooperation which the EU wants to embody.

Even in the field of social policy which is so much part of the national welfare state, attempts have been made to transcend national borders. The Treaty of Rome was still an exclusively economic affair, leading up to the establishment of the European Economic Community, the EEC. But in 1974 the EEC launched the first "Social Action Programme" dealing with such items as industrial relations, working conditions, equality of men and women as to access to employment and training, and so forth. One year later a "Poverty Programme" was inaugurated.

In the 1980s this social policy focus was intensified together with the determination to implement a single European market by the year 1992. Two documents highlighted this turn towards a transnational, European social policy: "Social Dimensions of the Internal Market" (1988) and "Community Charter of Fundamental Social Rights" (1989). The latter, incidentally, had a strong labor orientation and dealt with workers only, not with "ordinary" citizens, many of whom were unemployed. It should be noted also that right from the beginning the United Kingdom refused to authorize these and similar documents. It was opposed to transnational, European social policies since they were considered a matter of national sovereignty. Moreover, the conservative government, in power during the 1980s, rejected the predominantly left-of-center arrangements which continental welfare states tried to include in these transnational projects. Nevertheless, pressures to extend the EU's legal competence to the social welfare field led to the inclusion of a "Social Chapter" in the "Treaty of the European Union," drafted in Maastricht 1992. The ratification of this treaty by the parliaments of the members states led in several cases to severe political problems.

The "Social Chapter" of "Maastricht 1992" set out to implement the "Social Charter" of 1989 but added various new items: "the protection of workers when their employment contract is terminated, conditions of employment for third-country nationals residing in Community territory, financial contributions for promotion of employment and job creation, and the integration of persons excluded from the labor market."[4] It was proposed also to eventually set up binding directives which would formulate the minimum requirements for a gradual implementation of the "Social Chapter." It is needless to repeat that the United Kingdom rejected all this forthwith.

Will all this eventually lead to a transnational, borderless European welfare state? The EU has an open border policy which aims at a free traffic of persons, goods, and services within its territory. A group of nation-states—the Benelux, Germany, France, and later also Italy, the original signatories of the Treaty of Rome—decided to go ahead with this plan and signed the Schengen Treaty. As of 1 January 1993 there is a free traffic of persons between these nations, which means that there is only minimal border control between them. The Schengen partners decided to guard the outer borders of the Schengen area in a uniform manner and to apply the same uniform policy to refugees asking for political asylum. In the pursuit of criminals, policemen may transgress the inner borders of the Schengen area.

Meanwhile, these Schengen measures, intended to precede a EU without inner borders, has run into considerable obstacles. France, for example, has refused to open its borders with the Benelux, claiming that a very busy, illegal traffic of drugs takes place between Rotterdam and Lille. Much to the chagrin of Dutch politicians (and citizens as well) a high-ranking French official labeled Holland a *narco-état*. This was enough to trigger sentiments of nationalism and "euroscepticism" among the Dutch who generally believe that their drug policies, intended to decriminalize drug addiction and to distinguish, if it comes to legalization, soft from hard drugs, are superior to those of most surrounding nations—those of France in particular, where allegedly percentage-wise drugs and drug addiction are a much larger problem than in the Netherlands.

While the "europhiles" and "eurosceptics" are quarreling, the borders between the European nations have more or less been erased in the

world of higher education. Various degrees have been mutually acknowl-
edged. The EU finances scores of programs in which students and scholars are exchanged. Countries with minority languages, such as Holland,
Denmark, or Flemish Belgium offer graduate programs in one of the
major European languages, mostly English. Although higher education
has always been prone to transcend borders, particularly in research,
the EU has strongly fostered the advent of a truly borderless higher
education. In this context, the European University Institute at Flo-
rence functions as a model of borderless higher learning. Needless to
say, modern electronic technology adds to the advent of a borderless
intellectual community, a truly international republic of letters. Much
more radically and rapidly than the telephone and the fax, e-mail, and
the Internet penetrate deeply into societies, even if these societies, like
Communist China, try to prevent their intellectuals from participating
in the free exchange of information and ideas.

In sum, as to borders the welfare state presents an interesting case.
Prior to 1980 its operational limits were geographical by nature and in
this respect quite strict. But, as we have seen before, its internal operational scope seemed to be limitless. Within the confinements of national
borders and jurisdictions most Western European nations erected comprehensive welfare states. As to the extension and intensiveness of their
welfare programs, only the sky seemed the limit. After 1980 things
were almost the reverse. The geographic borders of these comprehensive welfare states opened ever wider, while their internal operational
scope became more limited and narrow.

Are we headed for a borderless, transnational, European welfare state?
In my view this is neither feasible, nor desirable. Despite the many
modernizing forces which foster a certain degree of uniformity, national differences forged by centuries of history will remain forceful in
Europe. It does not take much "euroscepticism" to conclude that a further surrender of national sovereignty, in the field of social policy as
well, will eventually be opposed strongly by the populations of the
various member states. Close cooperation is one thing, surrender of
sovereignty is something entirely different.

But there is another objection to a European welfare state. It is an
endogenous trend in any welfare state to centralize its power and to
establish, through massive regulation and legislation, a system of strong
and voluminous bureaucratic control. The welfare state is, as we have
seen, by its very nature an interventionist institution. If a European
welfare state would come about, we could expect a bureaucracy in Brus-

sels which would be infinitely more powerful and voluminous than it is already today. The national civil societies and markets would be greatly stifled which would gravely undermine the legitimacy of this would-be European welfare state. One does not have to be a "eurosceptic" to abhor and reject such a project.

Plurality of Welfare Regimes

However, the main obstacle a European welfare state would face is the empirical fact that there are in Europe several, incommensurable social policy regimes which will be hard to harmonize within one uniform system. The Scandinavian sociologist Gosta Esping-Andersen distinguishes three different worlds of welfare capitalism and consequently three different welfare state regimes.[5] He begins with the political premise that the welfare state is essentially a system of stratification which, with more or less successful results, liberates citizens from dependence on the forces of the capitalist market. (Rather cryptically for a reader not well versed in Marxist jargon he calls this "decommodification.") He then divides the world of welfare capitalism into three regimes: liberal, conservative, and social democratic. Various nations are clustered accordingly. The first regime around which Esping-Andersen groups the United States, Canada, and Australia, is a liberal welfare state "in which means-tested assistance, modest universal transfers, or modest social-insurance plans predominate. Benefits cater mainly to a clientele of low-income, usually working-class, state dependents."[6] Work ethic sets the moral standards, as a result of which dependence on welfare is being stigmatized. This type of regime, Esping-Andersen adds, minimizes the "decommodification-effects."

Continental European nations like Austria, France, Germany, and Italy, represent the conservative regime. A strong corporatist and etatist legacy shaped this particular regime, which from the start lacked the liberal preoccupation with market efficiency and dependency, and was not opposed to the granting of social rights to its citizens, particularly if that would help to avert social unrest among the lower strata of society. However, rights, including social rights, were attached to class and status. In particular the powerful, corporatists interest groups, state officials included, benefited from the non-universalist welfare programs, especially in the areas of education and pensions. In this regime, the traditional family is considered and treated as the basic welfare-receiving unit, while the subsidiarity principle, propagated and cherished by the Catholic Church, insured noninterference on the part of the state as long as the family is capable of serving the needs of its members.

The third, social democratic regime, around which the Scandinavian countries and the Netherlands are clustered, is defined by Esping-Andersen as "a welfare state that would promote an equality of the highest standards, not an equality of minimal needs as was pursued elsewhere."[7] This surely is a comprehensive welfare state: "the manual workers come to enjoy rights identical to those of salaried white-collar employees or civil servants; all strata are incorporated under one universal social insurance system, yet benefits are graduated according to accustomed earnings. This model crowds out the market, and consequently constructs an essentially universal solidarity in favor of the welfare state. All benefit; all are dependent; and all will presumably feel obliged to pay."[8]

Esping-Andersen's typology according to the three ideological mainstreams is, of course, rather crude. Incommensurate regimes are jammed together into these three slots. In addition, as we observed earlier already, his typology is itself rather ideological. More helpful in this respect is the distinction of four, geographically separate regimes by Stephan Leibfried. He distinguishes a Scandinavian, a Germanic, an Anglo-Saxon, and a Levantine variant.[9]

In the *Scandinavian regime*, exemplified most clearly by Sweden, welfare policy is based on full employment and not on the redistribution of wealth through strategies of income transfer. Not so much social security but participation in the working process is the main objective of the Scandinavian welfare state. The state is the main employer, in particular for women, and subsidizes both the (re-)entry into and non-exit from the labor market. Here the aim is a universalist, work-centered society. Thus, this type of welfare state is generous, if there is the will to participate in work, although it is quite strict and severe, if mentally and physically healthy people try to avoid work.

In the *Germanic regime*, exemplified first and foremost by Germany and Austria, but in many respects by Holland as well, quite a different strategy unfolds. Leibfried calls it a compensatory regime. The state tries to "pay off" social problems, subsidizes the exit from or even non-entry into the labor market, and pursues a policy of economic growth simultaneously. In view of unemployment, the right to social security is easily substituted for the right (let alone the obligation) to work. It stands to reason that a universal basic income irrespective of having work or being unemployed, is seriously debated, if not yet realized.

Increasingly this compensatory regime abandons means-testing and its orientation is towards the individual rather than the household.

The *Anglo-Saxon regime*, as realized in the United States, the United Kingdom, Australia, and New Zealand, can be typified after Titmuss as a "residual welfare model." Like the Scandinavian regime, the Anglo-Saxon welfare state envisages a "work society," yet it does so by coercive mechanisms, not by subsidies, or trainings and qualification policies as in the case of the Swedish welfare state. The Anglo-Saxon model of residual welfare is, of course, far removed from the Germanic regime which, as Leibfried argues, comes close to "a universalized, non-residual needs approach."[10]

Finally, there is the welfare model of what Leibfried calls "the Latin Rim Countries," preferably labeled the *Levantine regime*. It is exemplified by Spain, Portugal, Greece, and to a certain extent Italy as well, in particular its southern part. In these countries, a rudimentary welfare state remains. They sometimes resemble Anglo-Saxon residualism, implementing in actual fact forced entries into the labor market. Yet, older traditions of welfare, often stemming from the Roman Catholic Church, persevere which are alien to the Anglo-Saxon tradition. Moreover, strong agricultural biases persevere and there has never been a tradition of full employment, as in Northern European countries. There are, Leibfried concludes, constitutional promises of a "modern welfare state," but the legal, institutional, and social implementation is in general lacking.[11]

Thus, apart from the often strong reluctance to yield important portions of sovereignty to "Brussels," it is—given these different welfare state models and stemming from very old and thus persistently different traditions—not very feasible that a European welfare state will emerge. Leibfried also draws this conclusion: "In my view, all European development will most likely leave all poverty and welfare policy at the local or state—that is, at a sub-European—level.... The common ground is missing on which a European welfare regime could be built."[12]

This is, however, not to say that these nationally different welfare states will carry on the interventionist centralization that has been so typical of the comprehensive welfare state. Stockholm, Paris, the Hague, Bonn, and Westminster have been, despite all the differences in welfare regimes and despite an often strong civil society, the epicenters of political power and social policy during the heyday of the welfare state. This has changed because ever since roughly 1980 the capitals of these welfare states have been obliged, for economic as well as political and sociocultural reasons, to yield much of their bureaucratic power, on the one hand to the EU in Brussels, and on the other to lower authorities, the large cities in particular.

As to the latter, national centralization will in all probability not be endangered "top-down" by a prospective European welfare state, rather it is increasingly put under "bottom-up" pressure by urban and regional developments. In most European countries not the EU and Brussels but rather regions and cities have thoroughly shaken the centralized and bureaucratized structures of the intensive and extensive welfare state of the 1960s and 1970s.

Regionalism

Jacques Delors spoke of "l'Europe des régions, pas des nations." The Europe which this former, trend-setting chairman of the European Commission envisaged was not a centralized and bureaucratized union of nations but rather a federation of regions that shared common cultural, social, and economic features and interests. Not rarely did such regions transcend national borders which in many cases are already historically contingent. Delors added to this idea of *euroregions* the old Catholic idea of *subsidiarity*: higher administrations should not aspire to perform what lower administrations are perfectly able to do. In many respects regional authorities can, in this vision, function more efficiently and effectively than national governments and "Brussels," since they usually heed more readily the social, cultural, and economic interests of regional citizens and regional public as well as private organizations. Needless to add, this notion of regionalism which is growing in popularity within the European Union, has grave consequences for the postwar welfare state to which we grew accustomed. It deserves closer scrutiny.

It is regrettable that there is a considerable degree of vagueness as far as the concept of region is concerned. There are, to begin with, undefined differences in geography and size: Western, Northern, Eastern, Southern, and Central Europe are often called regions, but so are Wales, Scotland, Northwestern Germany and Southern Germany. Euro-experts using the concept often view it one-sidedly as an economic phenomenon. Particularly regions in Southern Europe, and after 1989 in Eastern Europe, are viewed as areas in need of economic development, comparable in a sense to developing countries outside the EU. So-called *euroregions*, or *euregions*, have again a different size and scope. They are regions that transcend national borders and view themselves as unities because of shared economic interests and traditional sociocultural characteristics. There is, for instance, the euroregion "Maas-Rijn" which covers the Dutch, German, and French-Belgian area between Maastricht, Aachen, and Liège.[13]

There are, in conclusion, also *ethnoregions*, as exemplified by Wales, Scotland, and Catalonia which view and define themselves beyond common economic interests in terms of culture and identity: shared history, language or dialect, customs and idioms, religious beliefs, and practices, and so forth. Their political conception of region comes close to the concept of nation. Consequently, this type of regionalism strongly resembles nationalism.

In any case, regions and regionalism are at odds with the idea of a welfare state whose power and authority is centralized in the capital of a nation-state with distinct geographic and political borders.

Socio-scientific and political concepts are, of course, not constructed and applied in a vacuum. Changes in the social, cultural, and political environment do affect such theoretical and political constructs. We, therefore, must face the question to which extent the recent developments in Europe—its laborious but progressing economic, political and maybe even sociocultural integration, the spectacular collapse of communist systems in Eastern and Central Europe, the resurgence of ancient nationalisms and ethnic hatred, etc.—compel us to rethink and reformulate social scientific concepts and theories. Is our present socio-scientific language still adequate, when we employ basic concepts such as "state," "welfare state," "nation," and "nation-state" without much reflection about the changes the European continent experienced recently—changes which have by far not come to a conclusion yet?

The Scottish sociologist David McCrone addressed this problem in a study that bears the significant title *Understanding Scotland: The Sociology of a Stateless Nation* (1992). The concept "society," McCrone argues, has been used until now in a rather generalized and uncritical manner without much regard for the historical and cultural specificities of distinct nations. In sociology "society" usually means "social system," "industrial society," "modern society," or "capitalist society." Whenever and wherever societies modernize, the usual argument is, they develop into a social system, an industrial society with common features that produces sociological and even political convergences. This led to the belief that there is indeed a general sociology which is allegedly adequate to analyze and interpret nations that are historically and culturally rather different. American sociology, for example, has been adopted in the past decades as "modern sociology" by Europeans for whom it represented some sort of model sociology. McCrone questions the legitimacy and the adequacy of this type of thinking which obviously holds that sociology is some sort of culturally neutral pastime, whereas it obviously is not. The abstract and rather unsociological idea of a general sociology precludes a true understanding of the social and cultural incommensurability of specific nations.[14]

The generalized and rather abstract notion of "society" has a conceptual runner-up, i.e., the notion of the "nation-state." In fact, McCrone argues, state, society, and nation are usually employed as equivalent and equally abstract concepts. As a result, British sociology that deals with the social structures and processes of the British nation-state has always been believed to be adequate and heuristically useful for a sociological understanding of such distinct historical and cultural entities like Wales and Scotland. This McCrone contests strongly. Scotland, he argues, has been and still is (since the formation of the British state in 1707) a socially and culturally distinct entity—a nation, albeit a nation without a state. In order to fully understand Scotland, a sociological analysis and interpretation is needed which views it not as an abstract entity, not as part of an alleged "modern society" which is always in the end "British society" conceived of as a nationwide welfare state. What is needed is a sociology of Scotland as a stateless nation.[15]

McCrone, I should emphasize, is not in favor of a nationalistic sociology. On the contrary, he warns against a one-sidedly cultural approach that focuses primarily on Scottish traditions, and looks more to the past than to the future. He is, in other words, not in favor of some sort of tartanized sociology: "the search for a pure, national culture as an alternative is doomed to fail in a complex modern, multinational world."[16]

This is not the place for a detailed critique of McCrone's ideas. One could, of course, question the validity of his position, which is tinged with the postmodernist predilection for historical contingencies, social and cultural fragmentation, and the alleged end of Enlightenment rationalism which contributed so much to the ideas of a nation-state and a welfare state. The postmodernist deconstruction of the Enlightenment has indeed focused on the state as an allegedly outmoded and outlived institution. In an essay that is as forceful as it is fateful, Jean-Marie Guéhenno indeed announced the end of the state as being the end of democracy.[17] It reminds one of the days of the Weimar Republic, when a comparable, nearly postmodern fragmentation, stricken by scores of contingencies, heralded the end of democracy but also—and this postmodernists should heed—the beginning of one of the most cynical dictatorships history ever witnessed.

In addition, McCrone's Scotland-specific sociology, although it probably will not slip off into reactionary nationalism, might very well produce a kind of intellectual provincialism which is at odds with the processes of political internationalization and economic globalization. One of the attractive components of the Enlightenment was not only its focus on a borderless market but also on the dream of a transnational *republic of letters* in which there would be an exchange of ideas unhampered by social, economic, cultural, and geographic borders. Nation-specific sociology and policy would in all probability put an end to such a transnational republic of letters.

If the European Union would indeed realize the basic principle of subsidiarity, leaving sufficient socioeconomic and political room for various, vital civil societies and their specific (urban, regional) cultures, it could very well function as a transnationally institutional framework for economic regions, euroregions, and ethnoregions, in other words, stateless nations. Culturally, the EU will then also function as the institutional foundation for a European republic of letters, enabling artists, students, scholars, and journalists to meet and discuss in a rational, reasonable, and critical manner. The EU, we just saw, will and cannot assume the functions of a welfare state, but it can function as a *cultural marketplace* in which not just people, goods, and services but ideas, ideals, values, and norms are exchanged to the enrichment of all parties involved.

In sum, during the 1980s and early 1990s the EU developed beyond its originally economic scope into a socioeconomic, perhaps even cultural, entity[18] in which regions, not nations or nation-states, prevail. In the process national welfare states have gradually lost their former enclosure by the political and geographic borders of the nation-state. This contributed to their fragility and vulnerability. And since the comprehensive welfare state depends on strong centralization, regionalism and its call for subsidiarity which both are contrary to centralization, corroded the very foundation on which it has rested. In sum, this process contributed forcefully to the waning of the comprehensive welfare state as a postwar institution.

The Urban Culture of Poverty

Throughout history, cities, as Jane Jacobs in particular has argued particularly convincingly, have been the main sources of the wealth of nations.[19] But throughout the ages big cities have also been the seed-beds of grave social problems like unemployment and unemployment-related poverty, and crime and crime-related addiction. Even in its heyday, the welfare state has not been successful in its war on urban poverty and destitution. Although the concept has been severely criti-cized in the past by socio-scientific researchers, it can hardly be denied any longer that the big cities of Europe and America are particularly conducive to a *culture of poverty*. In this culture, which is passed on to next generations, poverty and the informal or even criminal ways to cope with it, are accepted as "normal" and "unavoidable." In this cul-ture *anomie*, as defined by Robert Merton,[20] seems to be the rule rather than the exception. If ultimate goals like affluence and security cannot be realized by formal-legal, bourgeois "normal" means, they are pur-sued informally and illegally. Those who do not follow these paths of crime, and they are in the majority, will easily fall prey to the passive ethos of amoralism.

Obviously, the welfare state has not been successful in its attempts to reduce poverty effectively, let alone to eradicate it. Large sums of money poured into cities and troubled neighborhoods have been to no avail, like seeds sown in rocky soil. On the contrary, many welfare state programs and services seem to reinforce the culture of poverty. It took some time to realize two basic facts: first, culture—the culture of poverty—has contributed to the persistence of urban poverty and mis-ery; second, welfare state programs and services have contributed un-intentionally to the persistence and tenacity of this culture.

It is obvious that unemployment ought to be singled out as one of the main causes of urban poverty. Non-accessibility to a regular job and a steady income is, to many analysts, the beginning of a downward spiral. But the problem is that there is no simple chain of cause-and-effect at play. If a culture of poverty exists, it is as much the effect as the cause of social and economic destitution on the part of specific categories of people. Welfare may alleviate the worst poverty of the unemployable or structurally unemployed, but it also reinforces the ties of dependence which reinvigorates the culture of poverty.

The single-parent household, for example, is currently singled out as an important cause of socioeconomic misery and as an important source of urban, drug-related, juvenile crime. To many boys and young men the gang acts as a substitute for the family, the gang leader a substi-tute for an absent father. However, poverty and crime in the big cities are, in a sense, also the cause of the single-parent family; this is statistically illustrated by the fact that single-parent households constitute the core and bulk of urban poverty and welfare dependence. In view of this vicious circle, or downward spiral, most socio-scientific debates about urban poverty and the policies to fight it are rather senseless. They usually stem from a single cause which however is in most cases also an effect.

In any case, the centralized, interventionist welfare state has not been succesful in eradicating urban poverty and related urban anomie. On the contrary, the welfare state unwittingly fostered anomie by making the recipients of welfare services dependent on professionnals and bureaucrats. Welfare dependence holds people hostage by a system built with good intentions. Since the welfare that is provided, particularly the substitution of income, remains at a minimal level, poverty is never really eradicated thereby reinforcing a sense of dependence and civic inadequacy. In turn this fosters the institutionalization of a culture of poverty. Indeed, urban poverty has become an institution.

It is typical of anti-poverty policies to focus on so-called welfare cases and meet their needs according to formal, bureaucratic categories and rules. This, needless to add, reduces welfare dependents' citizenship significantly. One is eligible for welfare services only if one belongs to a bureaucratically and statistically constructed category. Before one receives welfare benefits in the Dutch system, one is categorized and filed, and then kept within the bureaucratic limits of this category. In a sense one's citizenship is reduced to a number in a computer of the appropriate office. One is not allowed to acquire additional income through paid labor and receives distinct benefits by remaining within the category into which one has been put. Of course, those who are able to dodge the system and engage in "black labor," can acquire relatively extensive wealth. Many, however (in particular mothers on welfare in single-parent households) get caught in the system and are in a sense held hostage by it. In many of these cases, there is no way to escape the previously discussed downward spiral.

As the term "culture of poverty" suggests, this typically urban social problem ought to be seen and treated primarily in the "field" so to speak, in particular cities and specific neighborhoods, and *not* in the rather abstract and bureaucratic context of a comprehensive welfare state. A major problem here is that in such a strongly centralized context, cities have lost much of their capacity to operate administratively in an autonomous manner.

Indeed, in view of the many social and economic problems cities face today, the existence of a centralized comprehensive welfare state is a grave impediment. Even if governmental authorities are spread over three levels—the national (federal) government, the province (state), and the local community (city)—the tendency of the comprehensive welfare state has always been to absorb as much power and jurisdiction as possible. In the case of social policies this centralization was usually legitimated by the argument that only a nationwide welfare state could guarantee the equal distribution of welfare services and benefits. The comprehensive welfare state as a giant wealth-redistribution system was believed to prevent grave socioeconomic inequalities among various regions and cities within the nation.

Meanwhile this rather mistaken conception of the principle of distributive justice had an adverse effect upon the cities, and in particular upon their capacity to confront the grave social ills within their administrative realms. Their administrations became clogged with statutes and controls by the central government, not in the least in the area of welfare provisions. In a sense, the growth of the welfare state led to a steady decline of the city, while its administration lost concurrently the capacity and authority to tend to the specific needs of its citizens.

This lack of autonomy incidentally also prevented them from responding adequately to the economic competition of other cities within and beyond national borders.[21] In other words, the comprehensive welfare state did not only hamper the forces of competition in the market, but managed to impede also the competition among cities. In the 1980s it became abundantly clear that cities in comprehensive welfare state regimes were not in need of more money from the central state, but rather of more independence and autonomy.

The Need for a Vital Urban Culture

It stands to reason that an important component of the shaking of the comprehensive welfare state after roughly 1980, has been the resurgence of cities as sociocultural and economic entities which were above all in command of more autonomy and self-regulation. Indeed welfare state decentralization means in the first place a rather radical decline of "statism" or "etatism" and a corresponding rise in "urbanism," that is, in the administrative competence of cities, specifically big cities.

The phenomenon of *eurocities* deserves mention here. The twinning of cities and towns is an established, now worldwide, tradition. In Europe, this tradition has led to the emergence of large cities that consider themselves economic and sociocultural hubs whose radius of action transcends the borders of their nation-state. They present themselves and function, in actual fact, as European urban hubs, called eurocities. They do so largely on their own, without much interference from or influence by the central governments. In fact, the mayors of these eurocities travel through Europe and the world, like state ministers, or ambassadors of their cities, usually at the head of business delegations that negotiate important trade deals. Eurocities compete with one another in terms of economic performance, but also in terms of cultural activities in the arts and sciences (festivals, exhibitions, and conferences). The hosting of important sports events, too, is part and parcel of city marketing these days.

In the world of business, the notion of corporate or organizational culture became quite prominent during the 1980s. The basic idea is that particularly in view of global competition, product quality and quality of services are essential for survival. However, actual differences in quality are usually negligible in today's world. The quality one has to offer should therefore be communicated in terms of corporate identity. It is this identity, expressed through the overall corporate culture, that transforms the name of the corporation into an authoritative brand. More important, however, is the fact that a distinct corporate culture and identity inspires people in all ranks of the organization, binds them to the organization emotionally and thereby improves their performance.

The same is true of urban culture. After the emergence of European cities as influential political, social, and economic actors at the end of the Middle Ages, cities developed a specifically urban culture which has always been predominantly economic and civic. Free from feudal bonds, kinship ties, and rural (religious and magical) strictures the inhabitants of the early capitalist European cities cooperated in handcraft and trade; services like law, banking and insurance soon followed. They thereby developed a specifically urban culture and identity. This culture and identity was indeed the source of pride and solidarity which was very different from the traditional bonds of feudalism, religion, and kinship. The difference was above all that urban pride and solidarity were open, flexible, and in a sense remarkably modern qualities.

Urban culture was not just an economic culture promoting and promoted first by trade capitalism and later by industrial capitalism. It was as much a civic culture which fostered the political participation of its inhabitants and thus laid the early foundations of European democracy.

A feudal serf who managed to survive in a city for 101 days was freed from his feudal bonds and received urban citizenship. Also the bourgeois class would soon capture the most influential positions, and contribute to the urban class system. Needless to add, such an economic and civic urban culture contributed to the economic performance, as well as to the political power and autonomy of European cities.

Thus, urban culture, as an economic and civic culture, is crucial to the economic performance and political position of cities. The history of Europe has seen periods in which cities were characterized by strong urban cultures (cf. the Hansa League, and seventeenth-century Holland), and periods in which their cultures declined and grew stale and powerless. It stands to reason that a comprehensive, centralized welfare state which absorbs much power from lower authorities and functions as the epicenter of the nation's power and culture, does considerable damage to the autonomy and the identity of cities. In fact, urban culture has the tendency to dwindle, to grow stale, functional, and bureaucratic, under the regime of an intensive and extensive welfare state.

The danger of this situation is that it affects the economic performance of a city which ought to, on the contrary, function as a source of a nation's wealth. Instead, urban problems multiply. While corporations and affluent citizens turn their back on the city, poverty and crime rise. The Pavlovian response in the heyday of the welfare state was increased state intervention through scores of subsidies and attached rules and regulations. This "statism" hastened the decline of urban culture and the proliferation of its economic and social ills.

However, after roughly 1980, concomitant with the gradual curtailment of the comprehensive welfare state, we notice a resurgence in urban culture. Urban administrations, particularly those of influential eurocities, have become aware of the importance of urban culture as an economic and civic culture, not just as the core of city marketing, but also as the social and economic environment which potentially has salutary effects on the alleviation of urban problems like poverty and crime.

In short, one has become aware of the need to create an urban environment which inspires people to participate in urban affairs, to create neighborhoods which are safe to live in, to reoccupy the public space outside one's front door. For a long time this space has been viewed by politicians and civilians as a space for which exclusively the welfare state, its professionals, and civil servants, bore responsibility. Now public space has been "rediscovered" by ordinary citizens who assume responsibility for it. In Dutch cities this has become known as *Social*

Renewal which, in the end, is a process in which residents of streets and neighborhoods help themselves and each other to keep the street and neighborhood clean and safe. Social Renewal will be discussed further in chapter 5. For now it suffices to emphasize that this indicates a remarkable social and cultural transformation: urban residents are no longer prepared to let their neighborhoods deteriorate further, neither do they expect the city government, let alone the national or federal government to operate as the sole entity responsible for the solution of their neighborhood's social problems. In any case, the social revitalization of neighborhoods as a bottom-up process is an important precondition for a successful halt to the downward spiral of the culture of poverty.

The resurgence of urban culture in the cities of Europe plays a pivotal role in the deconstruction of the strongly centralized, interventionist welfare state. This renewal of urbanism in the big cities of Europe is fostered by, and in its turn contributes again to the steady decline of the top-down, abstract "statism" of the comprehensive welfare state.

Reconstructions

Even in the heyday of the European welfare state prior to the 1980s, care was never exclusively a statutory affair. On the contrary, in most established, Western European welfare states there was a regime of "welfare pluralism"[22] in which the market, the state, and civil society coexisted and functioned in conjunction. Thus, with respect to the market citizens could always privately buy (often additional) services and goods deemed necessary for their well-being (consumer goods, education, health care, etc.) and insure themselves against various risks through private insurance corporations. However, in a welfare state regime social services and income transfers will also and even primarily be arranged statutorily for specific groups and categories of citizens whose social (in some cases even constitutional) right it is to receive them. This is the public welfare system. Finally, even in a comprehensive welfare state there still are informal and mainly voluntary organizations, operating privately in society, yet often subsidized by the state in cash and through tax exemptions. An obvious example is the Salvation Army, which delivers goods and renders services to needy people.

As a sociological rule, the more extensively and intensively statutory welfare expands, the less influential the private market of care will be and the more the informal and voluntary assistance will decline. In fact, the ethos of the comprehensive welfare state is such that charity is frowned upon and rejected as old-fashioned and degrading dependence.[23] Naturally, the reverse is also true: when, for whatever reasons, the welfare state is reduced through decentralization, deregulation, and privatization, the market of commercial welfare and the voluntary services within civil society will regain prominence. It is often claimed that this is precisely what happened in Europe after roughly 1980. The claim is not totally wrong but needs some differentiation and qualification.

The 1980s have often been viewed as the decade in which the state was superseded by the market, whereas political and socio-scientific debates in the 1990s have focused on the reemergence and revitalization of civil society. However, political and socio-scientific attention has been directed primarily and predominantly towards the changing relationships between state and market, leaving those between state and civil society and between the latter and the market largely unexplored, certainly as far as social services are concerned. In fact, social services rendered by voluntary organizations in civil society are often shelved under the very insufficient category of philanthropy. Moreover, the activities of organizations in civil society that play an influential role in the affairs of the welfare state and the market, the trade unions and employers' associations, mainly, are usually categorized under the heading "corporatism." Left-of-center critics tend to interpret corporatist organizations as seedbeds of conservatism, and usually fail to acknowledge their eminently democratic function as mediating structures. The present analysis focuses on the strained balance of state and market in the waning of the welfare state after roughly 1980, and we will deal with corporatism insofar as it bears upon this balance and the changes thereof.

As to the shaky relationship between state and market in the areas of welfare and care, one should heed the warning that a decrease of public expenditures by various budget cuts is in itself not yet indicative of a fundamental change in the relationship in favor of the market. If, for instance, the Austrian welfare state cuts its budget drastically, it is important to know that a large share of its public spending consisted of benefits to privileged civil servants.[24] It is doubtful if such reductions in public spending will benefit the market, let alone ordinary citizens within civil society. There is, of course, also the possibility that reductions in public spending have been brought about by a more efficient and effective organization of certain statutory social services. In addition, the demands for social services on the part of citizens-customers are, of course, not constant and invariable. They can, for whatever reason, decline and thereby cause a proportionate curtailment of the supply. Finally, when the supply of statutory services declines, it is by no means certain that citizens will turn to the market for supplements.

Usually, Margaret Thatcher's and Ronald Reagan's policies are mentioned as examples of more-market-and-less-state strategies. Basic transformations did take place in the welfare states they intended to transform, yet the public expenditures of the United Kingdom and certainly those of the United States did not decline. On the contrary, public debt in the case of the United States rose to astronomical heights. It requires detailed historical and comparative budget analyses to find out when and in which programs expenditures declined and raised. Raises may be due to military expenses, declines at the cost of basic social securities and services.

It is interesting to observe how various right-of-center governments took command in most Western countries around 1980, or during the 1980s. They all promised to curb public spending and to stimulate the market. Naturally, this kind of turnaround could not be realized within a couple of years. But left-of-center critics usually emphasize the right-of-center ideological rhetoric, and claim that this well-meant intention to curb the national deficit did not at all materialize. An important part of the problem is, however, that the slogan "less state, more market" is deceptive. First of all, in order to bring about the envisaged turnaround of a comprehensive welfare state, one needs a strong, not a weak central government. This central government ought to reform first and foremost its internal organization and then shake up its bureaucratically stifled, dusty organizational culture. It must also come to terms with scores of compartmentalized interest groups within its own ranks and within civil society. In this coming to terms with interest groups it must focus upon the revitalization not just of the market but of civil society as well. However, there are very few concrete strategies by which a central government can exert positive influences upon civil society. It is easy to stifle civil society through overregulation and heavy tax burdens, but it is difficult to stimulate and foster it by direct and concrete policies. In short, it is quite a large order which can certainly not be realized in just a few years.

Meanwhile, all the signs indicate that in most comprehensive welfare states the decentralization of its power to lower authorities and the privatization of many of its functions and services, have indeed reduced the power of the central government's institutions. This has unmistakably fostered the revitalization of the market and its competing stamina. However, a large proviso must be made as to deregulation. If national governments made serious attempts at deregulation, the European Union seems to have "compensated" through an increase in supranational regulations. In any case, the waning of the comprehensive welfare state should be recognized in particular in the processes of decentralization and privatization. Naturally, policies as to the curtailment of the public deficit contribute also to the gradual decline of the central state's impact on the market and civil society:

> In his study on the welfare state in transition Johnson distinguishes five measures by which welfare state governments try to curb their public deficits. There is, to begin with, the lowering of the level of allowances like child support, unemployment benefits or social insurance benefits. In Germany, the Netherlands, and France such measures have been taken during the 1980s. Second, one can increase social benefits beneath the level of inflation with the effect that their real value decreases annually. England lowered its unemployment, child and illness benefits in this way. Similar measures were taken by the governments of Denmark, Norway, and the Netherlands. Third, almost all welfare states in Europe cut their expenses by sharpening the admission criteria of the various social services. Fourth, an individual contribution to the costs of certain services, or an increase of already existing contributions, in particular in health care, was introduced in England, Norway, Germany, and the Netherlands. The introduction in Denmark and the Netherlands of a certain period of waiting before the benefit would be dispensed, contributed also to budget cuts, particularly in the area of sick leaves. Fifth, the reduction of the number of civil servants too contributed to the shrinking of the welfare state. According to Johnson, this reduction was very sizable in England, but it can be witnessed in other welfare states as well.[25]

The (very ambiguous and ideologically heavy) notion of *corporatism* plays a crucial role in socio-scientific analyses of the welfare state transformations after 1980. A society is generally called corporatist, if there are powerful societal organizations which operate in the political arena and in the market as interest and pressure groups. The most influential of such organizations are the trade unions and the employers' associations, the collective bargaining of which determines much of the social and economic policies, guaranteed and legalized by the government and the parliament. There are national and historical differences. Thus, Austria's corporatism is by and large the result of the Roman Catholic Church's grip on societal organizations, whereas Dutch corporatism has been shaped by its tradition of pillarization. Swedish and Danish corporatism have other historical origins. But they all have this in common: major processes of decision making, particularly as far as material and immaterial welfare is concerned, cannot take place successfully if representatives of social interest groups were excluded from it. Thus, in order to be effective, social policies depend on mutual consensus. Corporatism is usually viewed as being conservative and therefore conducive to stagnation and averse to innovation. Neo-liberals like Margaret Thatcher and their social democratic opponents share this aversion to corporatism.

Liberals and social democrats usually fail to see and understand such corporatist organizations and institutions as mediating structures between individual citizens and the state. The mediation, as we have known it since Tocqueville and Durkheim, prevents on the one hand the overpowering of citizens by an omnipotent, powerful, interventionist state, and on the other hand the continuous and direct interfering in the affairs of the state by citizens propagating their private interests individually or collectively.

In any case, corporatism can and in many cases will slow down, or even frustrate an all too radical neo-liberal revitalization of the market, or an all too radical social-democratic interference in the affairs of citizens and business corporations by the state. It is, in a sense, the prerogative of conservatives to defend corporatist, mediating structures as the backbone of a vital civil society. One should bear in mind, for instance, that Thatcher's energetic rule did not end under pressure of the opposing Labor party let alone the weak Liberal party, but because of discontent within her own Conservative party. The rank and file of her party was generally satisfied with the fact that much of the trade unions' power, particularly that of the miners, had been broken. But to many conservatives it was quite unacceptable that lower, local authorities and related organizations of citizens, the core of conservative constituencies, were increasingly and in fact quite arrogantly set aside and overruled. Actually, corporatist power in England has always been much wider and deeper than trade union power. Despite the comprehensive welfare state scores of rather old intermediary associations have remained influential in British society, perpetuating British culture, its class structure in particular. However, these traditional and often rather conservative bodies functioned simultaneously as buffers between the power of the state and the influence of the citizens, smoothing and softening the impact of both of them.

The recent success of the Dutch economy, fruit of rather stern policies in the 1980s, is in this respect an interesting case. Liberals and Social Democrats were inclined to decry the traditional intermediary structures in civil society, obvious remnants of pillarization, as representatives of a sticky, traditionalist and conservative corporatism. Gradually, however, the insight gained ground that these mediating organizations, the unions and employers' associations in the first place, generated a societal consensus and trust which have been very conducive to a well-functioning market. It contributed in particular to a pervasive flexibilization of labor and the labor market. In the heyday of the comprehensive welfare state one was certain of a steady job with many social benefits, but very uncertain of work after a lay-off. Today, one is certain of work with flexible contracts and few social benefits, but it is difficult to get a fixed, tenured job. The risks of this rather American labor model need to be covered increasingly through private insurance. The system has proven successful; its blooming economy is testament to this. Whereas unemployment was still rising in the middle of the 1990s in France and Germany, it has steadily declined in the Netherlands since the start of this decade. It is called the Dutch Polder Model for which the foundations were laid in the 1980s, when the comprehensive welfare state was steadily dismantled.

Health Care Reform and Hybrid Organizations

Next to education, health care has always been one of the most crucial sectors of the modern welfare state. Knowledge and thus education is, of course, increasingly important in fully modernized societies, whereas physical and mental health has grown into one of the most essential values of modernity. Indeed, our preoccupation with health is a remarkable cultural phenomenon which conditions our acting, thinking, and feeling and which is, of course, very fertile and profitable soil for medical and paramedical therapies and therapists. The steady greying of Western societies contributed also to this preoccupation with health since, of course, health conditions worsen in old age. All this gave rise to the ever growing and expanding power and influence of medical professions which, as we saw before, established within the welfare state sizable and powerful interest groups with an equally sizable professional dominance.

Meanwhile, due to this new focus on health and the concomitant increase in health care demands this sector of the welfare state began to experience unprecedented annual expansion. There is, in terms of public spending hardly any sector of the welfare state which can compete with the health care sector, while the demographic perspective of a rapidly greying of society predicts even stronger growth in this sector.[26]

Therefore, if it comes to a reduction of state deficits, most welfare states began with reforms of their health care system. Very few have been successful. There are mainly two reasons for this failure of health care reform. The first reason was the simple fact that health and health care are to the general public very sensitive subjects and thus difficult for politicians, who ought to heed the sensitivities of their electorate, to tackle. Secondly, in the past very intricate and complex legal and organizational arrangements for health care and cure have been set up which cannot be easily transformed, reformed, or removed. Needless to add that the various professional groups in the medical world exert rather strong pressures since their interests are at stake here. After all, they have strong cards in their hands, because they deal with matters of life and death. One thing seems to be apparent, however, large, comprehensive health care reform plans are doomed to fail, politically as well as socially.

But there is still another reason for the failure of reforms of statutory health care systems. This rather formal and highly bureaucratized system has lost its monopoly. Since the 1980s informal and commercial systems have emerged and are still spreading in the seams of the formerly comprehensive welfare state. Not only private health insurance but also commercial health care provisions are slowly but gradually spreading. Informal care by voluntary (non-profit) organizations and by families, friends and neighbors—still unheard of in the heyday of the comprehensive welfare state—is also again on the rise. Even traditional philanthropy and charity, as exerted by organizations like the Salvation Army, are reappraised these days.[27] Naturally, there are significant differences from country to country. In Sweden these developments are quite modest still, in the United Kingdom they are more substantial.[28]

Very recently the Dutch government initiated legalization that intends to put an end to private hospitals, which have emerged modestly in the recent past alongside the very extensive public health sector. It proves that the lobby of public hospitals is a forceful and influential one. It proves above all that there are still strong and powerful remnants of the comprehensive welfare state of yesteryear at work here. The argument used is, of course, that a dual system of health care in which affluent people and workers of powerful organizations can dodge the usual waiting lists of the public health sector, is not acceptable. Competition in the field of health care is thus curbed, if not completely eradicated.

As this incidence demonstrates, the state often still retains a considerable regulating and financing role despite much rhetoric about decentralization and privatization. After all, there is generally still a lot of public money involved in such hybrid semi-public, semi-private organizations like the public transportation companies and the postal services. There are in particular many mild forms of privatization, such as the contracting out of services for which the state remains ultimately responsible. Market dynamics can be strengthened within the statutory domain by compulsory competitive tendering of services. In the public health care system of Great Britain tendering of nonclinical services like cleaning, catering, and laundry has become quite customary. At the end of 1985 almost 24 percent of the nonclinical service contracts had been awarded to external companies.[29] In this way and also through tax reliefs on private pension schemes, mortgages, private health insurance or school fees, the welfare state is still kept intact.[30] It is for this reason that concepts like "quasi-markets" and "quasi-nongovernmental organizations" (quango's) have come up.

Indeed, also outside the health sector one may expect in the near future a growth of such hybrid organizations which are semi-public and semi-private, controlled partly by the state and partly by the market, bearing a peculiar culture in which the market orientation of business administration is mixed with a bureaucratic ethos. It is more than rhetoric and newspeak, when staff members of the health care system talk about the people they serve not as patients but as clients, while officials in city hall often address citizens as the consumers of their services. It is for better of for worse a remarkable change of culture.

It can be expected that formerly comprehensive welfare states like Sweden and the Netherlands will shy away from drastic and radical reforms of their welfare systems. They will rather focus on various forms of close cooperation between the public and the private sectors, between statutory and market insurances and provisions. The formerly sharp borders between the public and the private will blur, which will cause the emergence and spread of scores of hybrid, semi-public, semi-private organizations. It will certainly reinforce the complexity of these societies, hamper their transparence, and in all probability increase and augment social and economic risks. The comprehensive welfare state was, due to its abundant regulations not very transparent but it did present most citizens with a sense of security. In fact, to some this type of society and culture had probably too few risks and incentives to offer.

But living in these formerly comprehensive welfare states nowadays is, on the contrary, for many citizens a rather risky business.[31]

Customers in the Market for Social Security

There is a solution other than this piecemeal fading of the borders between public and private sectors which gives rise to hybrid organizations like the quango's and to scores of risks and insecurities for the citizens. We could transform the system of welfare insurance and services such that the individual citizen is no longer a passive subject of state regulations and state-controlled provisions but an active consumer who is able to buy the needed insurance and services as on a market of care and welfare.

The basic idea of a welfare state is that citizens bear a collective responsibility for the equally distributed social security and welfare of all. This is the moral principle of solidarity. But, as we saw before, this principle grew stale and abstract, and thereby lost much of its legitimacy.

It stands to reason that the system carries what has been called the *moral hazard*: it invites people to use the system for the benefit of one's own, private interests. If one's income is insured even in the case of light illnesses, it is attractive to feel ill and stay away from work for some days. Since one does not bear directly the financial burdens of medical treatments, the "consumption" of medical services and of medicines will increase easily and steadily. In 1992 the comparative percentages of working days which were taken off for sick leave were indicative: Sweden, 11.6 percent; Germany, 8.8 percent; the Netherlands, 7.7 percent; France, 7.1 percent; Italy, 6.3 percent; Belgium, 6.1 percent; Great Britain 5.8, percent; Denmark, 5.2 percent; the United States, 2.9 percent; and Japan, 1.6 percent.[32]

It does, of course, not make much sense to moralize about the moral hazard and the abuse of the system by individual citizens. It has, therefore, been argued that people ought to be made more cost aware and this can allegedly only be done by showing them concretely that in the end their own pockets suffer when insurances and provisions are abused. One way of doing this is the well-known *voucher system* which could and is being used in the health and education sectors. Apparently, however, this system seems to illicit quite a massive bureaucracy if it is to function well.

The Hannover Chamber of Commerce has presented a different system in which also a change of behavior and mentality on the part of the citizens is envisaged. It is a change from *recipient* of welfare dispensed by a welfare state to *customer* in a market of welfare provisions supervised by the state but run in a competitive manner. The proposal deserves closer scrutiny as it is indicative of the change of thinking about welfare and welfare state services in Europe these days.

The author of the report, which bears the title "From Welfare State to Social State," emphasizes that the proposed change of welfare distribution is not a demolition but a fundamental reconstruction of the welfare state. Citizens are transformed from passive recipients to active consumers of welfare who remain personally responsible for their own welfare. The core of the welfare state, it is argued, consists of four types of insurance: (a) continuation of income or salary in cases of illness by the employer; (b) health insurance; (c) unemployment insurance; and (d) pension plan. In Germany, it has been calculated that the last three insurances (contributions by employers and workers) cover 39.3 percent of the gross income. This was only 26.5 percent in 1970. In the industrial sector the costs of the continuation of income is on average 4.9 percent.[33]

The report proposes to place these often sizable contributions by employers and workers in *private social accounts* by which the worker buys the necessary social insurance as he himself sees fit. There is, of course, a compulsory minimal insurance so as to prevent irresponsible behavior by people who refuse to insure themselves or chose to remain underinsured. They may end up drawing on the dole for which, of course, the community will eventually pay the costs. But beyond this minimal insurance, individuals are at liberty to insure themselves and to do so in the market of private insurance companies. They are equally free to insure themselves extensively and intensively, spending most of their social account, or be more careful and economical and thereby save on the social account. These savings may come in handy later, for instance when one is in need of special and expensive care in old age.

There are, of course, scores of intricate problems which such a change has to confront. For instance, if pensions are also included in the social account, there will be a necessary period of transition in which one generation has to carry the burdens of two generations—not just those of the aged, as is the case now, but of itself as well.[34] The latter will be the case the moment the social account system is instituted. An additional contribution, this report claims, will be unavoidable for the duration of this transition period. It could be compensated, he believes, by the savings in the social account on the part of the other three components. This, it seems, requires a considerable amount of solidarity and moral discipline from the workers concerned. Still there is the looming problem of the structurally unemployed and the unemployable. They are unable to set up their own social account, and must therefore somehow be taken care of by the traditional welfare state.

In any case, if one sets out to reduce the collective expenditures of the comprehensive welfare state and the moral hazard it necessarily entails, without endangering the basic social security of its citizens, this proposal deserves serious consideration. It can, however, also be applied in a less neo-liberal, individualistic manner. City governments, for instance, could install social accounts for specific neighborhoods from which they would finance the public services needed to keep their streets clean and safe. Naturally, in that case the citizens in these neighborhoods need to organize themselves to this end. Through a tender system they could then buy the cheapest and the best services according to their own collectively expressed wishes. It would contribute to a bottom-up democracy and strengthen the concrete sense of public responsibility on the part of the people who live in the neighborhood and use its public services.

Conclusion

As these and other ideas and proposals indicate, the heyday of the comprehensive welfare state is over. There is a different social and political climate in those European societies which were until recently in the grip of the comprehensive welfare state.

What then will happen in Europe in the next decades? Will there be a growing convergence between the minimal welfare state systems of most of the United States on the one hand and the transforming welfare states of most of Western Europe? Or shall we witness a steady divergence between the two continents as far as welfare and social security are concerned? This would certainly be the case if a European welfare state, orchestrated by and from Brussels, emerges in the foreseeable future. As argued before, such an event is not very likely. The cultural diversity of the European continent is, despite the modernizing forces which often neutralize cultural differences and distinctions, too strong to believe in the future viability of sociocultural uniformity.

Many social scientists and commentators claim that philosophical and moral differences are too apparent to believe in a future convergence of the welfare systems of Europe and America. Allow me a well-nigh ritual citation of Albert's idea of an unbridgeable gap between two kinds of capitalism: the American brand which is hectic, short-term, in the end socially insensitive and irresponsible, and the Western European, Rhinelandish brand which is perhaps slower, but heeds the long-term perspective and tries to remain responsive to the needs of people, in particular marginal and marginalized people.[35] As I said before, it is questionable whether this obviously very ideological, and, I am inclined to add, typically French, contraposition of Europe and America is very helpful, when one tries to understand the social policies of either one.

Predictions as to socioeconomic and cultural developments are always hard and hazardous. However, if I venture to draw conclusions from the developments discussed in the present chapter, I believe that the near future in Western European societies will not witness grand, planned and systematic changes of the welfare state but rather piecemeal, yet influential transformations. If anything, recent failures on both sides of the Atlantic to change health care systems in a comprehensive and grand manner should give rise to modesty and prudence. Again, I rather expect incremental changes and transformations of the welfare state which in the end will lead up to more fuzziness as to the distinctions between the public and private sectors, more flexible interfaces among the state, the market, and civil society. This will undeniably cause more insecurity and complexity, and thus a greater awareness of risks and maybe even more anxieties. But it will also generate unsuspected and mutually profitable collaborations between the three cornerstones of democracy—the state, the market, and civil society. In that respect, American and European societies will not differ greatly, because although there are in terms of social policy different historical origins and cultural traditions, they both aspire to be and remain vital democracies that function socioeconomically within a civilized brand of capitalism. This unites them just as it simultaneously separates both of them from many other nations in this world.

Notes

1. It has been suggested that in all probability economic and political refugees, and low-skilled members of ethnic minorities, two categories which at present are seen as grave financial burdens, will be needed to fill in the gaps in the younger cohorts of most Western European societies.
2. There were, of course, various liberalist and conservative critiques of the welfare state, as for example voiced by economists like Hayek and Friedman, but they were in general not accepted and seriously taken into account by the bulk of sociological analysts.

3. For this and other information in this section I made use of *Welfare in a Civil Society*, Report for the Conference of European Ministers Responsible for Social Affairs, United Nations European Region, Bratislava, 28 June– 2 July 1993. Published by the European Center for Social Welfare Policy and Research (European Center Vienna), Vienna, 1993. See in particular pp. 5–25, 48–65.
4. Ibid., p. 114.
5. Gosta Esping-Andersen, *The Three Worlds of Welfare Capitalism* (Princeton: Princeton University Press, [1990]1993).
6. Ibid., p. 26.
7. Ibid., p. 27.
8. Ibid., p. 28. Usually, the following difference between the Swedish and the Dutch welfare state is emphasized: the former focuses on full employment and is strict as to the demand to accept a job even if it is below the level of skill and education, the latter, on the contrary, focuses on the equal distribution of payments and entitlements to prospective beneficiaries of welfare state services. However, all this has changed dramatically since the 1980s.
9. Stephan Leibfried, "Towards a European Welfare State? On Integrating Poverty Regimes into the European Community," in Zsuzsa Ferge, Jon Eivind Kolberg (eds.), *Social Policy in a Changing Europe* (Boulder, CO: Westview Press; Frankfurt am Main: Campus Verlag, 1992), pp. 245–80.
10. Ibid., p. 252.
11. Ibid., p. 253.
12. Ibid., p. 255.
13. There are grave obstacles on the road towards such transnational euroregions. These obstacles are in particular of a social and cultural nature. This was described and analyzed in a Dutch Ph.D. dissertation, which I supervised. See Cobi van Beek, *Samenwerking? Er zijn grenzen!* (Cooperation? There are Limits!), (Rotterdam: Barjesteh, Meeuwes; Tilburg: Syntax Publishers, 1996). The book contains summaries in French, German, and English.
14. David McCrone, *Understanding Scotland. Sociology of a Stateless Nation* (London: Routledge, 1992), pp. 1–15.
15. McCrone endorses the postmodernist view that the nation-state as a product of modernity approaches its end, making room for "a new trans-societal order." It would, of course, foster the autonomy of stateless nations. McCrone, ibid., p. 9.
16. Ibid., p. 13.
17. Jean-Marie Guéhenno, *La Fin de la Démocratie* (Paris: Editions Flammarion, 1993).
18. The idea of a unified European culture is usually rejected as an impossible, or undesirable dream. As an antidote to this by now conventional opinion one should reread T. S. Eliot's essay "The Unity of European Culture" which he published as an Appendix to his *Notes towards the Definition of Culture* (London: Faber and Faber Ltd., 1[1948]1962), pp. 110–24.
19. Jane Jacobs, *Cities and the Wealth of Nations* (London: Penguin Books, 1984). See also Jane Jacobs, *The Economy of Cities* (New York: Vintage Books, 1970).
20. Cf. Robert K. Merton, *Social Structure and Social Theory* (Glencoe, IL: Free Press, [1949]1964, 9th ed.), pp. 131–60 ("Social Structure and Anomie") and pp. 161–94 ("Continuities in the Theory of Structure and Anomie").
21. I discussed this in greater detail in *A Theory of Urbanity: The Economic and Civic Culture of Cities* (New Brunswick, NJ: Transactions Publishers, 1998).
22. See Norman Johnson, *The Welfare State in Transition: The Theory and Practice of Welfare Pluralism* (Brighton, Sussex: Wheatsheaf Books, 1987). Cf. also Warnfried Dettling, *Politik und Lebenswelt. Vom Wohlfahrtsstaat zur Wohlfahrts-*

gesellschaft, ("Politics and Life World: From Welfare State to Welfare Society"), (Gütersloh: Verlag Bertelsmann Stiftung, 1995).

23. See Robert Whelan, *The Corrosion of Charity: From Moral Renewal to Contract Culture* (London: IEA Health and Welfare Unit, 1996; Choice in Welfare series no. 29). In "the comprehensive, rights-based, cradle-to-grave welfare state," Whelan argues, "the very word 'charity' began to acquire the unpleasant connotations which still linger on." Ibid.., p. 61. He demonstrates how most philanthropic organizations of Great Britain, which have a respectable history, have been in fact absorbed by the welfare state through subcontracting and lavish subsidies. They thereby lost much of their voluntary nature and transformed gradually into semi-statutory bodies.

24. G. Esping-Andersen, *The Three Worlds*, p. 19.

25. Johnson, *The Welfare State in Transition*, pp. 150–77.

26. See for a survey of health care provisions in various welfare states see Norman Johnson (ed.), *Private Markets in Health and Welfare* (Oxford: Berg Publishers, 1995).

27. See Robert Whelan, *The Corrosion of Charity*.

28. Ibid., pp. 1–15.

29. Ibid., p.21.

30. Ibid., p. 11f.

31. Cf. Ulrich Beck, *Die Risikogesellschaft: Auf dem Weg in eine andere Moderne* (The Risk Society: The Road to a Different Modernity), (Frankfurt a.M.: Suhrkamp, 1986).

32. Wilfried Prewo, *Vom Wohlfahrtsstaat zum sozialen Staat* (From Welfare State to Social State), (Hannover:Industrie- und Handelskammer, 1992), p. 21.

33. Ibid., p. 10.

34. The system by which the younger, working generation pays for the pensions of the older, retired generation is, of course, growing into a huge problem nowadays because of the greying and degreening processes. In the past the Netherlands has set up a different system for its many state employees: the pension contributions by employers and workers have been placed in a pension fund which by now is the largest in the world and, of course, a giant institutional investor in the stock market. It would be interesting to apply the private social account system to this fund: it would run empty, but individual civil servants would suddenly receive sizable contributions to their private accounts.

35. Michel Albert, *Capitalism against Capitalism* (London: Whurr Publishers [1991]1994). The gnostic, or Manichaean nature of Albert's essay has remained, as far as I know, unnoticed. This, and its naive acceptation by most academics, journalists and politicians, is more worrisome than the self-congratulatory animus, which permeates so many European expositions that deal with America critically.

5

Morality and the Democratic Triangle

Beyond the Comprehensive Welfare State

Before the velvet revolution of 1989 the citizens of Central and Eastern Europe experienced the suffocating grip of a totalitarian and bureaucratic state which stifled the market and lamed civil society. After 1989, a strong anti-state animus emerged, and many had great expectations of a truly free, democratic society. One had, in particular, high hopes and expectations of a free market in accordance with the classical liberal model of capitalism. It would, one expected and believed, yield prosperity for all in a short time. Certainly in Eastern Europe, as we know now, the chain of events turned out to be quite different. The polity is in chaos, the economy still in shambles, and civil society suffers from a very deep anomie. The voids are filled up by corruption, organized crime, atavistic sentiments of nationalism and its natural ally, racism. Part of the recent war in Bosnia was so-called ethnic cleansing, a cynical word for ethnic genocide.

One thing seems to be abundantly clear: in a situation like this, in which the central government has failed to gain trust and legitimacy, in which the economy remains structurally weak and civil society anomic, it would be disastrous to focus one's policy solely on one of the three pillars of democracy—the state, the market, or civil society. Economic advisers tend to stress free competition, and generally try to minimize the role of the central state and other regional and urban authorities. They leave, moreover, a blank space as to the role and relevance of organizations and institutions in civil society. That is a tragic mistake. Some advisers envisage a welfare state model in which the mechanisms of the market are curbed by the state. Here too, civil society is often treated as a residual category. Others again have the tendency to overemphasize the importance of mediating structures in civil society, while they usually minimize the importance of a free market and the necessity of a coordinating, stimulating, and controlling state. In short, what is really needed, if one wants to bring about a viable democracy in formerly communist countries is a policy approach in which the three corners of the Democratic Triangle—state, civil society and market—are kept in the balance.[1]

Although much less dire, this need of a balanced Democratic Triangle is also existent in Western European nations in which the extensive and intensive welfare state has by now run its course. These were, of course, not totalitarian societies and their central bureaucracies did not control and stifle the market and civil society to the extent this had happened in communist regimes. Yet, it became clear after the oil crises of the 1970s that the extensive and intensive welfare state could no longer be maintained economically, and that its expanding, predominantly bureaucratic control had a socially and morally adverse effect on civil society. A radical reconstruction of the welfare state, it became ever more clear, was due. Privatization, decentralization, and, though less successful, deregulation were the central processes of this reconstruction. Their aim was to revitalize the market, but also to revitalize civil society in which citizens could conduct their civic lives in autonomous organizations and culturally vibrant institutions. Only in such a vital and vibrant civil society can the values, norms, and meanings, which provide the lives of people with direction, certainty and security, and which fosters trust and solidarity, prosper and grow, keeping the democratic house away from the abyss of anomie.

Ever since 1980, things have happened in the formerly comprehensive welfare states of Western Europe that indicate a reinstitutionalization of the Democratic Triangle. Sure enough, there are voices which preach in a prophetic tone "the end of democracy" and "the end of the nation-state." Others fear the disintegration of both the state and civil society, and the spectacular rise in corruption, organized crime, and nationalist separatism. These are indeed serious and realistic prospects in these decades of transition. But there are also observable and demonstrable developments and processes which rather point in the direction of a re-institutionalization of the Democratic Triangle. Policies ought to be in line with these developments and processes and stimulate them by all means available.

It stands to reason that the quest for values, norms, and meanings—broadly speaking: morality—occupies a central position in the decline of the welfare state and the re-institutionalization of the Democratic Triangle. The comprehensive welfare state was, as we saw, a technocratic, one-sidedly functional-rational megastructure in which an immoralist type of ethos prospered, an ethos which in turn fostered the operations of the welfare state again. But with the waning and shrinking of this technocratic megastructure this type of ethos also lost much of its predominance. Naturally, its historical contrast, the moralist type of ethos, regained strength and stamina. It is this remarkable, yet rarely discussed change in morality, so crucial to the re-institutionalization of the Democratic Triangle, that deserves further attention.

This turn towards moralism will be dismissed by the last adherents of a radical welfare state, in particular by its socio-scientific ideologues. If it comes to morality and moralism, these critics usually refer to "the stifling 1950s" with suffocating mechanisms of social control and an oppressive morality borne by the petit-bourgeois, suburban, nuclear family. Yet, whether one likes it or not, it can be observed in several developments of the state, the market, and civil society that people are in search of values, norms, and meanings—that is, morality—which may give direction and steadfastness to their thoughts, emotions, and actions. It is short-sighted (if not arrogant) to see this only as a return to the days before the reign of an extensive and intensive welfare state— the 1950s. Apart from the fact that this decade was much less oppressive, petit- bourgeois and boring than the last afficionados of the welfare state and its immoralist ethos think or want to believe, the developments towards morality in the state, the market and civil society are in this way misinterpreted and fundamentally misunderstood. These developments are not a return to the past but herald, on the contrary, a new era in which the comprehensive welfare state is succeeded by a morally supported Democratic Triangle

Morality and the Market

The concept of "market" is, of course, hazy. Here is not the place for a discussion of semantics. The concept is used here, admittedly, in a superficial and not very sophisticated manner. It suffices to indicate its general meaning: the economy, or the economic system but also what is often called endearingly "the business community." Economic organizations and institutions, above all, the corporation with its staff and line are included.

In the nineteenth century two ideologies emerged which had very idiosyncratic and very influential views on the relationship between morality and the market. Both of them continued to influence socioeconomic discourses and policies until deeply into the twentieth century. The classic Marxist view of the market is that it is a capitalist institution and, as such, the main source of human misery and degradation. Competition sets the rules of the game, and since there is in capitalism a structural inequality as to the possession of the means of production, competition equals exploitation of those who only have their labor to sell in the market by those who possess the means of production. With regard to morality, the system of a free market is in this view pervasively and abjectly immoral.

The other view of the market is the classically liberal one. In this view the market is a morally neutral institution in which not moral agents but the invisible hand of competition rule. And as is always the case with ideologies, the true liberal believes that this basic fact is also a political norm: the market is best left alone and to its own devices. State intervention is necessary in monetary issues (as in the fight against inflation) and in moments when a defense against outside aggressors or competitors is called for, but should never meddle in the affairs of the market proper. The market is, according to the classically liberal view, not completely amoral, since one ought to conduct business, even in the most competitive of situations, in a gentlemanly and therefore fair manner. Indeed, *fair play* is a typically liberal component of market morality. Moreover, throat-cutting competition practiced by robber barons may be profitable in the short run, but in the long run it affects one's own interests negatively. Competition is like hunting, the favorite pastime of traditional liberals: it should not degenerate into poaching, and although the hunter's respect for animal rights is minimal, it is never totally absent. Thus, in the classically liberal view, morality is in the marketplace not absent but it is consciously held to a minimum.

The Marxist view which experienced a brief revival in the late 1960s and early 1970s has until now not played any role of importance in the reconstruction of the economy during and after the shake-up of the comprehensive welfare state. Apart from a few crypto-Marxist social scientists, most politicians and economists have embraced the liberal view. This was *a fortiori* the case in Central and Eastern Europe where Marxist theories had lost each trace of legitimacy already long before the collapse of communism. At times it is as if economic advisers and politicians in formerly communist societies have discovered a "new" gospel, the free-market gospel according to Adam Smith—an Adam Smith, incidentally, stripped of the very core of his thinking: moral philosophy.[2]

Meanwhile, in the Western world neo-liberalism has altered its approach of the market, away from amoralism ("objectivity," "value-freedom") or minimalistic moralism ("fair play") towards a more complete moralistic ethos. This was very apparent, for example, in the area of business administration where from the early 1980s on the phenomenon of *organizational culture* has attracted much attention, among academics in business schools, as well as among business administrators. It did not take long before the issue of *business ethics* was added to this topic. Courses in business ethics were added to the curricula of business schools and began to rank high on the agendas of business leaders.

This sudden interest in organizational culture is more than just another fad, and it is certainly more than a facile moralism on the part of business leaders. On the contrary, a couple of concrete causes can be pointed out. First, the remarkable rise and successes of Japanese corporations after World War II could not be explained solely by superior strategies and organizational sophistication, because the techniques of business administration in Japan were and still are compared to Western techniques, far from perfect. Apparently, the cultural factor, as exemplified in particular by a solid loyalty towards the organization one worked for, had to be singled out as the most explanatory variable. In addition, not quantity, output and immediate profits but quality, quality control and long-term results were the cornerstones of Japanese corporate strategy, and that too had much to do with the cultural factor. In short, organizational, corporate culture was viewed by most observers as the essential variable in the success story of the Japanese economy. Incidentally, one usually failed to realize that this corporate culture was intrinsically tied to the Japanese culture at large, and could therefore not just be imitated in a Western, American, or European context. But that is not our concern here. It suffices at this point to mention the fact that Japanese corporations demonstrated to Western observers the importance of the cultural and moral factor in the market.

During the wave of takeovers and mergers in the 1980s, business administrators ran into the cultural factor as a very hard factor, not, as the conventional wisdom of business administration had held it before, as a soft factor. Initially, takeovers and mergers took place after sound financial and organizational comparisons of the two concerned organizations had been made. In other words, one looked beyond the dotted lines of the respective accounts, and investigated the possible mutual fit of the respective formal structures. But then, after the takeover or merger had become a fact, troubles began. It often turned out that the cultures of both organizations—that is, the ways of acting, thinking and doing things, the mentality of the people who, of course, *are* the organization—had been quite different, so different that scores of mutual misunderstandings hampered the basic processes of communication and thus the proper functioning of the organization.

Organizational culture gradually became a very dominant element in the corporate strategy of the business community. The fact was (re-)discovered that workers in all the divisions and layers of the organization—now called "human resources"—performed much better, if they would view and experience the organization they worked for as "their" organization, as something to relate to meaningfully, to feel at home in emotionally, to be proud of and to identify with. In other words, the organization, business administrators began to realize, should be a meaningful order, a *nomos* which is infinitely more than just a production machine, as it had always been defined in Taylorism and Fordism. Sociologically speaking, the corporation was viewed increasingly as a *moral* reality based on values, norms, and meanings.

Naturally, the view of the market and marketing techniques changed accordingly. Today one realizes in most production sectors, particularly in the electronics market, that the quality of the products of different companies no longer differs much. Differentiation of products is, in terms of quality, increasingly marginal. This compels producers to focus their marketing strategies on the communication of their products as components of an idiosyncratic culture. Products need to radiate a corporate identity, need to show a "face," a brand name. Thus, next to and in line with corporate culture *corporate communication* developed into an essential component of business administration. The goal of marketing is to establish one's product in the market as a *brand* whose name is fixed in the consciousness of millions, like the names of celebrities in the worlds of entertainment and sport. The brand name is an extension piece, a billboard if you will, of the particular culture that is characteristic of the producing corporation. This too is, in a distinct sense, a turn towards business morality.

In the late 1980s and early 1990s still another turn towards morality occurred in the marketplace: *corporate governance*. Corporations with Stock Exchange quotations have come under special pressure lately. Not long ago the presentation of the annual account at the annual shareholders' meeting was in most cases a non-event, attended by individuals who in general were not very critical vis-à-vis the annual account presented by the board. And if these individual shareholders were critical, they missed the power to correct the board of the corporation. This has, however, changed with the advent of large, institutional shareholders, such as banks, pension funds and insurance companies. With the retreat of the welfare state pension funds and insurance companies have recently increased their capital considerably; this trend will continue in the coming decades. Much of this capital is, of course, invested in stocks. These and other institutional investors possess considerable portfolios in various companies, and are not prepared to deal with that through continuous buying and selling on the stock market. They prefer to keep these stocks as long as possible in the companies in which they invested them. Therefore, they want to be sure that these interests are taken care of properly by the board. The annual account (not so much the short-term monthly or bimonthly reports), and the internal and external audits are of critical importance to them, more so than to most shareholding private individuals whose interests in this or that company are minute in comparison to those of institutional investors.

All this is, of course, more than just a matter of correct and positive numbers on the dotted lines. In fact, it has, beyond sound financial management, much to do with *trust*.[3] Is this company with this president and board trustworthy? Do we entrust them our sizable interests? Trust, of course, is a moral quality that has much to do with a vital and healthy corporate culture and with clear and convincing corporate communication to boot. Increasingly, the annual account has become an instrument of public relations and of corporate communication. It should radiate vitality, originality, creativity—in short, a vibrant corporate culture as the moral foundation of trust.

Human resource management is, of course, part of this movement towards the cultural factor which, in the end, is a moral factor. This type of management focuses on an organization's most precious and indispensable asset, namely inventive, creative, active, and participative human beings. It is lately viewed increasingly as part of a larger phenomenon, called *social capital*.[4] At this point the market and civil society, which not that long ago were kept separate, merge. Social capital is usually defined as the capacity of an organization, or for that matter a society as a whole, to generate among its participants a clear sense of values, norms, and meanings which are expressed in scores of meaningful interactions and networks to the benefit of all concerned. Social capital is highlighted in particular by mutual trust. In Durkheimean terms, social capital is the opposite of anomie.

Social capital and trust, it is believed, is of prime economic importance, because it prevents high transaction costs. If people no longer relate to each other through meaningful interactions and networking, and if they are therefore unable to trust each other, they will formalize their interactions and joint activities by means of formal laws and bureaucratic rules. Oral agreements are in such an anomic situation null and void; they have to be corroborated legally by formal contracts. Meetings are held all the time, and successive meetings devote an inordinate amount of time and energy (and thus money) to the control and approval of the minutes of the former meeting. All this involves high transaction costs and yields very little profit.

Morality and the State

"State" is an ambiguous concept and its ambiguity is intensified in the compound word "nation-state," since the concept "nation" is equally multi interpretable. Again this is not the place to discuss definitions in detail.[5] Neither should it be the aim of the present argument to review the history of the state, the nation, and the nation-state as historical phenomena that are closely linked with the development of Western civilization during the past two or three centuries.[6] By "state" I mean the public administration which is usually divided into three layers: the central, provincial, and urban administrative authorities with their concomitant bureaucracies. (United States: federal, state, and local authorities; Germany: federal, *Länder*, and urban governments). State personnel is made up of politicians and civil servants, and constitutes what is usually referred to as the executive power. In a strict sense, the legislature and the judiciary do not belong to the state, yet in most modern democracies the two are so intertwined with executive power, the three of them making up the polity as a whole, that common consciousness views them as components of "the state" as well. This is certainly the case with the term *central state*, which is in everyday life connoted with "Washington," "Bonn" (soon "Berlin" again), "Paris," "London/ Westminster," and so forth. These governmental cities harbor the main institutions of the three powers of democracy.

Conceptual ambiguity increases again when the demarcation between polity and society evaporates, as is the case with the "welfare state." In daily parlance, but also in political and even in scientific debates it is not strictly the polity one has in mind, when one uses the words "welfare state." In actual fact, by "welfare state" the whole nation, including its society, its culture, and its economy is meant. One should bear in mind that this is not just conceptual sloppiness. The welfare state, certainly in its comprehensive phase, penetrated deeply into the market and civil society. It was for this reason that we defined it at the end of the Introduction as something which transcends the polity proper. It is, in other words, sociologically correct to view the welfare state in terms of polity, economy, and society.

Yet, when the concept "state" was used in the preceding chapters, it referred strictly to the administrative and public sector, consisting of governmental institutions and their bureaucracies. If we then want to determine what its relation is to morality, we ought to stress the fact that in a democracy the state is first and foremost a *constitutional* state— a *Rechtsstaat*—which has the *moral* duty to guarantee the safety as well as the political, civil and social rights of its citizens. If somehow this safety and these rights run the risk of being violated by internal or external forces, the state has to step forward, function as a shield, even if need be with the use of force. To that end the constitutional state has, in a democracy, the monopoly on violence through its army and its police force.

Within the context of postmodernism the end of democracy has been proclaimed or predicted, which is, of course, the end of the state.[7] The state, the argument claims, is a product of modernity, rationalized by the Enlightenment. It is narrowly tied to the nation as a discernible entity with geographical and cultural borders: the nation-state. But we have allegedly entered the postmodern era in which traditional institutions, like the church, the family, the university, the army, etc., with clearly discernible borders and limits, have run their course. We have allegedly entered a world of flexible networks, limitless contingencies, and virtual realities, without the grand and rational stories told by enlightened philosophers, scientists and statesmen.[8] Not rationality but irony is the mental capacity with which one ought to face reality—a multiple and increasingly virtual reality. In this postmodernist vision of the present world the state too has run its course. If it still exists, it does so as an increasingly virtual reality.[9]

However, to people in less fortuitous circumstances than the ones in which most self-proclaimed postmodernists live (in today's Bosnia, for instance, or in the underclass of the big cities), reality is not virtual but cruel, not multiple but depressingly uniform, not contingent but predictable. Moreover, even in an affluent and radically modernized society citizens constantly run the risk of being deprived of their most fundamental rights by aggressors, criminals, and scores of charlatans.

If the state as the final and most powerful guarantor and defensor of citizens' rights would whither away in a limitless ocean of amoral contingencies, flexibilities, and virtualities, these elementary rights would indeed be endangered. This would not just be the end of democracy, but the end of decent and civilized existence. In an interview an Israeli historian of Dutch descent vented his emotional dislike of the nation-state, which he saw as the main culprit of all the major miseries that have befallen mankind in the era of modernity. He looked forward to the days in which the state as an institution would no longer exist, and was even in favor of what he called "the privitization of violence." It would make a perfect context for terrorists and mafiosi, and when the interviewing reporter referred to the bombing of a federal government building in Oklahoma, he curtly responded that he would accept "a few Oklahoma's" annually, if we could get rid of the state.[10]

Three historical phenomena have greatly contributed to this mistaken view of the state which totally fails to acknowledge its moral nature as *Rechtsstaat*. First, it can historically not be denied that modern nation-states have contributed to the violation of basic human rights. This has happened, for instance, in colonialism which as a political and economic system did certainly not guarantee or defend the citizenship of colonialized people. In fact, some nations, even relatively small ones like Portugal and the Netherlands, managed to grow into globally powerful nation-states through the colonial domination of non-European peoples. As in the case of slavery, no valid moral justifications can be brought forward to the defense of the colonialist state. It contributed much to the negative image of the state which after World War II spread in most Western European countries.

Secondly, in the relatively recent past several modern nation-states in Europe grew into totalitarian systems which trampled upon the most basic human rights and abused the monopoly of violence in the most cruel of manners. Nazism and Stalinism come to mind as the most obvious examples. Again, no valid moral justification whatsoever can come to the defense of the totalitarian state. Its part in the history of Europe contributed much, needless to say, to the negative image of the state as such.

Thirdly, in a non-totalitarian and non-colonial manner the comprehensive welfare state which originally was envisaged as the prime guarantor of man's social rights, developed into a technocratic, value-neutral megastructure. Without totalitarian and colonial intentions by the parties involved, we saw before, the extensive and intensive welfare state "colonialized" civil society and the market, and held them in the semi-totalitarian grip of rules and regulations. It stands to reason that it became increasingly difficult to recognize any trace of morality in this type of overarching megastructure. The inherent decline of legitimacy contributed also to the negative image of the state as such.

However, these three causes of the by and large mistaken critique of the state as a constitutional institution are no longer at work. Colonialism came to its end in the 1950s and totalitarianism collapsed in Europe at the end of the 1980s. As to the comprehensive welfare state, as we saw before, it too has ever since the 1980s lost much of its prominence and centralized power. Decentralization, deconcentration, and above all the privatization of much of formerly nationalized services have led to a meaner, leaner welfare state. It has come to the point when European nations have to decide whether they want to maintain this reduced welfare state, or do away with it altogether. For moral reasons very few in contemporary European society want to abolish the welfare state entirely. In a civilized democracy, the common opinion is, the state remains invested with the moral task to guarantee and defend the basic social rights of citizens. To quote Beveridge once again, the welfare state as part of a civilized *Rechtsstaat* has the moral mission to insure people, in particular the most vulnerable, against "Want, Disease, Ignorance, Squalor, and Idleness."

Morality and Civil Society

In a sociological context, the sources of morality must be found in civil society. Again, this is not the place to debate possible definitions of this concept, which is at least as ambiguous as that of the state or the market. Civil society is defined here as the totality of associations (organizations and institutions) in which citizens conduct their lives socially and culturally, and through which they participate in political and market activities. It is, as we can learn in particular from Smith and Durkheim, within civil society that meaning can be experienced and values and norms expressed. Social behavior is more than merely biological conduct, it is meaningful interaction within a framework of values and norms. Therefore, social behavior is inherently a moral behavior.

Historically, the *bürgerliche Gesellschaft* (Hegel), or civil society, is the product of the trade-capitalistic cities that emerged at the end of the Middle Ages and the dawn of modernity. It gained economic and political prominence from the early modern period on. Civil society was and still is an urban phenomenon and finds its origin in the *bourgeois* class whose solidarity and moral power was not primarily founded upon kinship or magico-religious ties, nor on the possession of land, but on common material and immaterial *interests*. Pursuing these interests the *bourgeoisie* developed its very own and idiosyncratic associations and professions, and beyond that its very own and idiosyncratic urban culture. Urbanity grew into a specifically *bourgeois* style of life and mentality, bearing specifically *bourgeois* values, norms, and meanings. Within this context, democracy as a political system, capitalism as an economic system, and civil society as a sociocultural system emerged.[11]

The morality of the *bourgeoisie* contained some persistent values and norms which, even if they were derived from religion, as in the case of Puritanism, served to fortify and legitimate its political and economic interests. The work ethic, in particular, was a moral configuration of values and norms which undergirded scores of capitalist endeavors. To its functional orbit belong virtues like frugality, emotional control (rationality), and fairness. Not before long, the successful, rich and influential tradesmen formed a semi-nobility, the patriciate, and adopted values and norms belonging originally to the nobility. Of these bourgeoisified noble virtues courtesy and civility became the most influential ones.

Yet, value systems never exist in isolation. There is, as Max Weber phrased it, in the realm of values and norms an eternal "war of the gods" in which the good, nice, and beautiful of one system is the evil, unkind, and ugly of the other and vice versa. Or phrased differently, in the case of a dominant value system one will always find a counterpoint system which opposes the existing value dominance.[12] Thus, the type of ethos that we called "moralistic" will never exist without its counterpoint the "immoralist" ethos. In the Victorian era, for example, which in many respects was an era of moralism, immoralism and even decadence seemed to prosper as well. It was, after all, at the very same time also the era of Nietzsche and Wilde. Their ideas and lifestyles were not alien to the Victorian age, but a rather dialectical component of it, like the counterpoint that is part of the leading melody, harmony, and rhythm.

It may be a sociological prejudice but it appears as if civil society is the most crucial of the three corners of the Democratic Triangle, as it harbors and feeds the meanings, values, and norms that provide the other two corners, the state and the market, with vitality, creativity and a sense of direction. Civil society is in particular the breeding ground of social capital, i.e., of meaningful interactions, moral considerations, mutual trust. If civil society, for whatever reason, disintegrates into anomie, the Democratic Triangle is in peril as the state will dry up in bureaucratic formalism and repressive control, while at the same time the market will lose its stamina and augment its transaction costs. This state of affairs was exemplified by Eastern European nations prior to the collapse of communism. And, albeit much less radical, several Western European nations, we have seen, jeopardized their Democratic Triangle during the heyday of the comprehensive welfare state. In both cases, the greatest peril lay in the gradual disintegration and weakening of civil society as the main source of morality.

There is still another dimension in this relationship between morality and civil society which deserves closer attention. As was said before, civil society is the proper realm of mediating, or intermediary structures. The voluntary associations, in particular, in which citizens participate for the sake of shared interests, have functioned in the past as buffers between the individuals and their nuclear families on the one hand and the state on the other. Because of these buffers, power, in particular state power, is mediated and thus mitigated. Conversely, the influence of individual citizens too is in a democratic civil society never a direct influence, always a mediated, indirect one. This mediation and mitigation of power and, of course, its related force, contributes greatly to the civility of society. Indeed, due to this mediation the *bürgerliche Gesellschaft* is indeed a *civil and moral* society.

We have seen that one of the severest weaknesses of the intensive and extensive welfare state has been its almost innate urge to get a firm bureaucratic hold on both the market and civil society. As to the latter, we have seen that the comprehensive welfare state's spreading and intensifying etatism which—it must be repeated time and again—was not a totalitarian design but had been called for by almost all parties concerned, lamed the initiatives of citizens, made them dependent on the state, and thus increasingly blocked the functioning of voluntary associations. But also the nonvoluntary organizations and institutions, such as those in the fields of education, health care and leisure, gradually lost their mediating character and thus their buffering function. It has been observed and many times emphasized that the intensive and extensive welfare state threatened the vitality of the market because of its penetrative control through scores of rules and regulations. The fact that also civil society was affected negatively by it, generally has received less attention. The decivilizing and demoralizing effect the comprehensive welfare state exerts on civil society might well be a much graver and far more dangerous consequence.

Social Renewal

There is, however, no cause for alarm. As we have witnessed since roughly 1980, the days of the comprehensive welfare state are numbered. International, global developments, the rise and further expansion of the European Union, regionalism and urbanism, and, not in the least, the economically mandatory shrinking of the welfare state's scope of functions has led to a revitalization of the market and civil society. In Western Europe the revitalization of the market after 1980 was soon accompanied by the call for civil society's revitalization. In the Netherlands, for instance, the latter has been called *Social Renewal* and it has had its first, though still modestly positive effects, particularly in the big cities.

At the end of the 1980s the city government of Rotterdam installed a committee which received the assignment to formulate a concrete set of policies that would help to revitalize the urban economy.[13] When the committee delivered its recommendations most of which gave indeed direction to the ensuing economic policies of this city, the next committee was installed. It was asked to formulate recommendations for the revitalization of the city's social life. This social revitalization came to be known as Social Renewal. The gist of this committee's recommendations was simple but turned out to be quite influential.[14]

The various city streets and neighborhoods, the committee believed, had under the influence of the welfare state gradually changed their civic character. It was increasingly treated by citizens and politicians as an exclusively *public* domain for which the urban government and its allied professionals, not the urban residents, bore prime responsibility. For example, crime and safety have become everywhere a prime concern of urban residents and urban governments. The Pavlovian response during the heyday of the intensive and extensive welfare state was to view them as issues for which the state and the police bore the exclusive responsibility. In Social Renewal, however, safety and the prevention of petty neighborhood crimes (like burglaries and car thefts) are rather viewed as joined, public and private responsibilities. Residents can contribute to this by keeping the neighborhood clean and well lit, and by keeping a watchful eye on what happens in and around the neighborhood.[15]

In Social Renewal the role of the government is actually reduced to a conditional one: initiatives taken by residents to the effect that their streets and neighborhoods are made livable again, should not be frustrated by scores of regulations and controls customary to the welfare state. That is, when ordinary people in joint actions clean their street and neighborhood physically, and through stricter social controls socially as well, politicians, officials and welfare professionals should not stand in their way. This sounds simple but it means in terms of the welfare state a major cultural change. Urban residents have to reoccupy and reappropriate the public domain which they have abandoned in the recent past, and which was at the same time taken away from them by politicians, officials, and professionals.

Naturally the various projects reaped mixed results. In general the streets and neighborhoods that began projects of Social Renewal benefited from them. The involved residents enjoyed the often interethnic cooperation, felt a renewed sense of pride vis-à-vis their collective living space, and feelings of unsafety diminished. Yet, the process is not altogether free of problems. Continuity is obviously a major concern. In a modern society mobility is a ubiquitous phenomenon which makes it hard to count on steady involvement and participation of the people. There are legal obstacles as well. Recently, residents of a Rotterdam neighborhood fed up with drug dealers and buyers who are often "drugs tourists" from France and Belgium, took it upon themselves to badger these people, picketing notorious hang-outs and taunting prospective drug buyers. At the same time, however, they started in an abandoned house a special support program for young neighborhood addicts. It is a curious mix of force and civility. But there is a sizable additional problem. If residents are successful in pushing the drug "element" out of their neighborhood, it will move to the next one, as has happened before in the case of prostitution. What is obviously needed, is a chain of citizens' initiatives in the various streets and neighborhoods of the city. It requires citywide involvement and participation.

Naturally these residents were actually operating on the fringes of the rule of law. They, in a sense, touched the very foundations of the *Rechtsstaat* since they definitely used force which in a democracy is the monopoly of the state, that is the police. This is equally the case, of course, when residents hire private security agents for the surveillance of their neighborhood. It is a first step towards the privatization of violence which in a civilized democracy cannot be condoned. Such private security forces operating in the public realm should, if they are indeed necessary, at all times remain under the command and control of the police force, lest they develop into armed bands like the *Freikorpsen* in the fated Weimar Republic.

However, taking all of this into account, the revitalization of streets and neighborhoods, sometimes undertaken in joint interethnic efforts, is the main precondition for a successful attack on the major problems of big cities, particularly the inner cities. In former days the central welfare state and urban administrations as well have, at regular intervals, poured large amounts of funds and resources into urban renewal projects. On the whole these efforts have been of little avail. Not the residents, but officials, professionals, socio-scientific researchers and project managers were the main beneficiaries of such welfare state actions. The money was well meant but, in view of the minimal results, wasted. If the urban civil society remains in a state of anomie, the soil for social revitalization remains barren. No matter how many funds and energies one invests in it, it will continue on its downward spiral of anomie. Only the revitalization of the urban civil society from within can assure the success of urban renewal.

Therefore, it is not the state and certainly not the market but civil society itself that must turn the process of urban decay around. This smacks of Münchhausen's syndrome—tearing oneself from the swamp by one's own hair. But in a democracy that is precisely what people can accomplish. When among the residents concerned the will is there and the turnaround commences, the state as well as the business world can provide additional help by providing financial and moral support. In other words, what is needed for a successful Social Renewal is, beyond decentralization, deregulation and privatization, above all space for self-regulation, self-organization and self-financing by citizens. This modern specimen of self-help and not state-provided and guaranteed entitlements constitutes the basic social rights of citizens, the copestone of modern citizenship.

Obviously, Social Renewal equally means the restoration of some very basic moral links that had been severed during the heyday of the comprehensive welfare state: those between rights and duties, self-interest and justice, autonomy and responsibility, individual liberty and commitment, consumption and production. Come to think of it, Social Renewal is the precondition of a well balanced and vital Democratic Triangle.

Such a social regeneration runs into considerable obstacles in Central and particularly Eastern European nations, but they too will eventually witness the emergence of a free market and a free civil society. As to this prospect, there is a distinct difference between Eastern and Central Europe. Most of Eastern Europe has always lacked these basic freedoms, whereas the majority of Central European countries, certainly those of the former Austro-Hungarian Empire which was in this respect a remarkably enlightened regime, possessed at least vital civil societies and relatively vital economies. It was only after World War II that these liberties were trampled upon and suppressed by the forces of Soviet imperialism. After the collapse of this empire, these Central European countries could resume their civil society traditions. The most pertinent danger for these democracies is an internal one: they tend to emphasize in a one-sided manner the importance of a free market, neglecting the necessity of an equally vital civil society accompanied by a strong constitutional state. As a consequence, the imbalance imposed upon the Democratic Triangle creates room for corruption, organized crime, and atavistic nationalism. This is a very worrisome problem with which all post-communist societies must deal.

In most Western European nations, however, the revitalization of the market and civil society in conjunction with a retrenchment of the state could be effectuated much sooner and more smoothly. Here democracy, despite the fascist and Marxist contestations of former days, has grown into a solid tradition; and this even in the heyday of the intensive and extensive welfare state helped to maintain a considerable degree of positive and negative freedom in society and liberty in the market. Despite all the etatism that was engendered by the comprehensive welfare state, the voluntary associations, the organizations, and the institutions in civil society never suffered the severe loss of autonomy to which their counterparts in the communist world had been subjected. In other words, in Western European nations the market and civil society did not need to be created from scratch or re-erected after decades of totalitarian tutelage, they were just in need of thorough revitalization.

Once again, this revitalization of the market and civil society ought to be a reinstitutionalization of the Democratic Triangle. Morality—values, norms, meanings, and trust—is in all this a crucial variable. It should not be forgotten that the Democratic Triangle is first and foremost a *moral project* as it intends to balance a constitutional state which guarantees and defends the rights of citizenship, a free market which procures the material means of existence, and a civil society which through scores of free and mediating structures insures the full realization of citizenship. Maybe the rather technocratic and unimaginative welfare state of the past decades blinded us and made us unmindful of this basic fact?

Religion, Law, Arts, and Sciences

If civil society is the main source of morality, the question suggests itself what, in turn, is the wellspring of this civil morality. The answer is, of course, "culture," although culture in a strict sense, not in the broad, anthropological and sociological sense in which it was used above, when we spoke of national, urban, regional and organizational cultures. Culture in the strict sense is the concretization of the values, norms, and meanings of a distinct society in a given period of time. Culture in this strict sense is expressed empirically through the religious beliefs and practices of this society, but also through its laws, arts, and sciences. Thus, culture in the strict sense consists of religion, law, arts, and sciences.

The intensive and extensive welfare state had a distinct impact on culture in the strict sense of the term. As to religion, for instance, we have witnessed during the heyday of the welfare state a distinct loss of influence on the part of religious organizations. The comprehensive welfare state took upon itself a well-nigh providential role, in which it aspired to take care of the individual from the cradle to the grave. The French words for welfare state are in this respect indicative: *État providence*. Its services rendered the traditional, religiously inspired charity superfluous. It was replaced by state care. But in a sense the *État providence* replaced also the most fundamental element of religion: the alleviation of anxiety in the face of uncertainty. Who, after all, needs religious security, if the state provides a broad spectrum of social security and minimizes the material contingencies and risks of human existence? Meanwhile, since the technocratic welfare state lacked clearly defined and upheld values and norms, the material security it provided, remained devoid of a strong and guiding moral content. For instance, the intrinsic link between rights and duties, so relevant in most systems of religious ethics, was severed. As a result, the nonrational ethic of ultimate ends flourished while the rational ethic of responsibility withered away steadily.

Religious care and welfare is, of course, first and foremost moral as it is driven by religiously motivated values and norms. Religiously inspired philanthropy illustrates this fact. It stands to reason that this historically important source of morality, deeply entrenched in civil society, will be rediscovered, when the comprehensive welfare state retreats and loses much of its providential character. Contingencies and risks will unavoidably invade the daily lives of citizens and give rise to multiple feelings of insecurity and even danger. It stands to reason that this is fertile soil for religious experiences of sorts. Although this was not until now translated into a statistically relevant return to the established Protestant and Catholic churches, there is in most Western European societies a kind of re-religionization, which is the opposite of the secularization we had grown accustomed to when the comprehensive welfare state still took care of us.

We may conceivably also witness a revitalization of religiously inspired charity. Apart from the Salvation Army remaining remarkably intact, most religious charities became superfluous during the reign of the intensive and extensive welfare state. The same fate was suffered by the service clubs, such as Rotary, Lions, and Kiwanis. In Western European societies the service clubs changed their original, typically American mission of other-directed voluntary service to the community into a kind of inner-directed bundling of the mutual interests of the members. Projects of service to the community, after all, were the business of the professionals of the welfare state. Again, now that the comprehensive welfare state has run its course, we may expect a return of these European service clubs to their proper and original mission, which is voluntary service to the surrounding community.

One of the effects of the intensive and extensive welfare state has been that its legal arrangements acquired technocratic, instrumental idiosyncracies which entailed a severe weakening of their fundamentally moral nature. In fact, legality was in many respects essential to the comprehensive, interventionist welfare state, since its social policies had to be ratified by the parliament. But the greater amount of social legislation that passed parliament, the weaker the welfare state's legitimacy grew. Most ministerial departments of the interventionist welfare state, in particular those covering health, welfare and education, were under constant pressure to produce social and economic policies. As a result, they sent seemingly endless streams of laws and statutes for ratification to the parliament, after which they were then unleashed in society. In short time this particular legislation had become so incredibly complex that only a few experts could find their way through this jungle of rules, regulations, procedures, and legal arrangements. It was a truly inflatory process, and as is the nature of cultural inflation, all of these laws, statutes, rules, and procedures began to lose their meaning and thus their legitimacy. Thus, the more the legality of the welfare state increased, the weaker its legitimacy became.

This was exacerbated by the legal instrumentalism that took hold of this massive policy production. Laws and statutes were in fact no longer viewed and experienced as the proper democratic means for the realization and maintenance of a civilized, constitutional state, but employed primarily as efficient and effective instruments for the construction and maintenance of the comprehensive welfare state. Correct procedures are, of course, essential to democracy, but if they are transformed from means to goals they may lead to unintended consequences which in fact harm democracy.[16] This goal displacement rendered these laws, statutes and procedures unimaginative, technocratic, formalistic and meaningless.

Needless to add that after 1980, when the intensive and extensive welfare state was forced to retreat, the law and its statutes regained their original and fundamental nature as core components of a moral order—a true *nomos*—called democracy. The focus was no longer on a comprehensive and interventionist state but on the core business of the state as *Rechtsstaat*, as a constitutional state. This is not a return to the liberal, *laissez-faire* "nightwatch state" of the nineteenth century, but rather a concentration on the essential tasks of a national state which is politically located between the European Union and its expanding regulatory powers in Brussels on the one hand, and the increasingly decentralized powers of the regions *cum* cities on the other hand. The core business of the constitutional state is to assure the security and the human rights of its citizens, and to function as a shield for the socioeconomically vulnerable and weak categories among them.

As we have seen, the retreat of the comprehensive welfare state consisted, in main part, of deregulation and of privatization of public services. This had grave consequences for the world of law and statutes. First, deregulation means less centrally imposed legality and an increase in self-regulation and self-organization of citizens in civil society. This curbs the decline of legitimacy. Fewer laws and statutes simply means stronger, more convincing, and therefore more effective self-regulations and more initiatives on the part of citizens. Second, privatization means a gradual mixture of the public and the private spheres in society on the one hand and the market on the other. Again, this has consequences for the world of law and statutes, the most important of which is that legal regulations and arrangements come much closer to the needs and demands of customers than in the heyday of the welfare state, when the

law was being used as an interventionist instrument for the enlarge-
ment of the public sector at the expense of the private sphere.[17]

When, as happened in the Netherlands some years ago, the formerly
semi-public railroad system changes into a private system, travelers
may soon discover scores of differences. It is from their perspective a
mixed bag. Since the customary subsidies from the state have ended
and the system has to be run as a for-profit organization, prices will
increase and unremunerative services, mainly in the provinces, will be
closed. At the same time rules and regulations, and various services
offered to the travelers can now be designed and planned primarily for
the customer's benefit. Now railway companies must seriously compete
with the automobile, but it is in principle, if not in actual fact yet, also
subjected to the competition of rival railway companies. The Dutch
state owns the rail net and there is a small competitor who has received
a concession to operate on small portionss of this rail net. Profiting
from the open European market a French company expressed its interest
in this rival operation as well. In any case, the formerly monopolistic,
state-supported railway company is under heavy pressure to change its
modus operandi and its formerly rather bureaucratic and legalistic
culture. More than before, when the state acted as sole financier, step-
ping in whenever deficits had to be supplemented, the Dutch railroad
company will have to improve its service considerably.

This, of course, is much more than just a change in power structures
and decision-making processes, in financing procedures and processes. It is an essential change in mentality, in attitude—yes, in ethos, in
morality. From a technocratic amoral system that caused scores of
explicit and implicit immoral sentiments and actions on the part of
personnel and travelers, the system changed into a moral system in
which distinct values and norms make a difference.

This incidentally has moral consequences for the formerly wide-
spread habit of riding the train without buying a ticket. As part of a
state system, public transportation is easily experienced and treated as
an amoral, value-and-norm-free thing. It is then hard to experience the
"free ride" as an immoral, let alone petty-criminal act, simply because
it is hard to imagine that not-buying-this-ticket could contribute to the
eventual bankruptcy of the state. Naturally, it was precisely this "free-
rider" attitude and mentality, part of the immoralist type of ethos of the
welfare state, that contributed to the near bankruptcy of most comprehensive welfare states. However, if the railway system is a fully priva-
tized organization, the "free ride" carries a different moral weight. It

does endanger the continuity of the organization and thus the jobs of its personnel. Both travelers and train attendants will look at the "free rider" in a less immoralistic, easygoing manner.

Within civil society the arts are still another wellspring of values and norms. Contemporary artists and art critics are generally not inclined to view their lifeworld as a moral one. That was different in former days, certainly way back in Greek Antiquity, where beauty was experienced and pursued as both an aesthetic and a moral quality. There was a concept for this ideal expressed by the adjective *kalokagathos*—good and beautiful. In Renaissance humanism this unity of aesthetics and morality was rediscovered. The Enlightenment carried on this tradition, whereas Romanticism was inclined to couch aesthetics in an immoralist type of ethos. Yet, very few romantics would profess an amoralist view of art.

In a fully modernized context, such as the one of an intensive and extensive welfare state, which statutorily subsidizes the arts and artists for the purpose of safeguarding them against the competitive and risky market forces, the link between aesthetics and morality has been severed summarily. In fact, the comprehensive welfare state created economic sanctuaries for scores of *avantgardist* experiments in which even the most elementary notion of beauty, let alone morality, was abandoned. In many cases artists simply dictated to audiences, which were either baffled or enchanted by their experimental products, what they considered to be art and to be non-art. In this avantgardism for the sake of avantgardism both aesthetic and moral values were not allowed to play any role of significance.

But again, we have witnessed a turnaround also in the art world after roughly 1980, when the reduction of the intensive and extensive welfare state began. Apart from the decrease in state subsidies and the stricter norms for receiving those subsidies that remained available, artists and artistic organizations discovered the importance and necessity of nongovernmental private funds to be attracted through sponsoring and fund-raising. This rediscovery of the market and of market mechanisms would have been unheared of prior to the 1980s. Moreover, in the 1980s art and artists were in turn discovered by the corporate world where, for example, sponsoring of artistic events and the establishment of corporate art collections became customary again, as had been the norm in the early days of capitalism. Commitment to the arts developed rapidly into an important component of corporate communication as it contributed to the identity and the "face" of the corporation. Several corporations possess today important art collections. In sum, the corporate world has rediscovered the fact that art has potentially a cultural, qualitative surplus-value.

Many artists began to realize also that much avantgardism was comparable to a professionalism which increasingly catered to fellow artists and art critics in the name of an alleged artistic autonomy. During the days of state largesse very few of these modern artists realized or took to heart that in most cases the community had to pay for all this in the form of state subsidies. The general audience of non-professional art consumers was excluded from these avantgardist cliques, which of course reinforced again the neglect of modern art on the part of this audience. The result was a strong decline of legitimacy on the part of modern arts and artists.[18]

The Dutch comprehensive welfare state was once more a perfect example of this remarkable state of affairs. A system was set up in the 1960s by which the state in exchange for a monthly welfare allowance, collected nonmarketable art from artists and distributed it amongst its civil servants to be exhibited in their offices. The bulk of it, however, ended up in the depots of the ministry of social affairs and culture. Recent attempts to sell these art pieces for dumping prices were allegedly not very successful. In addition to this "contra-performance arrangement," as it was called, the state also subsidized the art world by declaring private purchases of contemporary art in commercial art galleries tax deductible.

All this began to change in the 1980s. State subsidies were reduced, and in the art world itself autonomous avantgardism was curbed. Remarkably and simultaneously, the awareness that market forces were at work in the art world occurred just as a sense of beauty returned to the arts. Atonal and serialist music passed its prime, as did extremely abstract, avantgardist figurative art. In addition, new audiovisual techniques brought about forms of art which were usually far removed from avantgardist autonomies. It was in fact a kind of electronic pop-art.

Meanwhile, the moral dimension remained intact. Museums, for instance, including those of modern art, began to attract more visitors. Apparently, museum visitors searched the arts for symbolic meaning, for realities that in a nonreflective and yet meaningful manner enabled them to transcend their daily life with its uncertainties, risks, and contingencies. The arts, it was rediscovered, present a sur-reality which potentially provides mundane reality with depth, meaning, and integrity. In this sense, artistic beauty regained not just its aesthetic but also its moral dimensions and qualities.

Finally, something similar happened in the world of science as well. The most successful scientific explanations of reality were, according to Copernicus, those that were pleasing to the mind.[19] This is, on first sight, a strange criterion, rather far removed from either verification or falsification, the two competing cornerstones of "true" science. Copernicus apparently found the aesthetic effect of a scientific theory of great importance: not catching the truth through experiments and logical deductions, but pleasing the mind through elegance was his main criterion of scientific success. Beauty, often described as the confluence of elegance and economy, was and still is an important criterion in scientific validation, but it was in its Renaissance origins paired, as is often forgotten today, to a moral criterion as well: in the end, science should contribute to the well-being and happiness of mankind. As no one else who stood at the cradle of modern science Giambattista Vico emphasized the intrinsic unity of reason and emotion, theory and practice, when he formulated his critique of Descartes and Cartesianism.[20]

Humboldt believed that science, whether viewed as *Naturwissenschaft* or as *Geisteswissenschaft*, should install in the minds and psyches of young people what he called *Bildung*. This concept is hard to translate. It is the capacity of mind and soul, a cognitive and moral quality which would help the individual to face reality in an adult and sovereign manner.[21] Although he made fun of German *Bildung*, John Adams had something similar in mind when he reported about his unending quest for *education*. He too meant a cognitive and moral quality that according to him could not really be acquired in the formal and traditional schooling of young people within institutional settings. On the contrary, Adams believed firmly in the educative capacities of life itself.[22]

Again, within the framework of an intensive and extensive welfare state education, often defined as life-long and permanent education, has been one of the main policy objectives. In fact, the largest portion of the welfare state's budget is usually devoted to the financing of primary, secondary, vocational, and university schools. However, the welfare state's main objective of formal education is the preparation of young people for the demands of the labor market. That is, education is primarily viewed in terms of vocational training. The welfare state, it is believed, should not spend considerable amounts of public money to subsidize the intellectual and moral growth of its citizens, as in the traditional ideal of *Bildung*. It ought to produce instead well-trained individuals useful to the welfare state itself and the labor market in general.

The sciences, in particular the social sciences, were put under pressure to focus on applied research useful to the construction and maintenance of the welfare state. Until the 1980s policymakers and social scientists alike believed in a sociotechnocratic manner that society could be rationally constructed and planned under the aegis of an interventionist state. If the welfare state possessed a dominant ideology, it was a technocratic kind of neo-positivism which believed firmly in the superiority of the applied sciences. The ideology has been called aptly *scientism* and its societal carrier was the previously debated Knowledge Class, or New Class. Apart from this normative belief in the value of the sciences, strong emphasis was placed simultaneously on the normative requirement that the scientific approach to reality ought to be value-free and amoral.

Protests against this kind of technocratic positivism did arise in the late 1960s and early 1970s, often in a neo- (or rather semi-) Marxist vein as in the Critical Theory of the so-called *Frankfurter Schule.* However, in general these protests were summarily neutralized by the welfare state, not in the least because most participants in these movements of protest were university students who upon graduation got jobs in the ever-expanding welfare state, or in the world of capitalist corporations, despite their flirtation with the self-proclaimed New Left, also called the New Class.[23]

In any case, prominent descendants of the contesting New Class have occupied and still occupy influential positions in the state ministries. As has been observed before, they were, despite their often loudly proclaimed protests against technocracy and capitalism, the "hidden technocrats" of the interventionist welfare state.[24]

It is interesting to note again just how much the climate has changed after 1980. In the succeeding decade it became clear that the schooling of the next generations, from primary schools to higher education, ought to encompass more than merely "training." Education in the true sense of the word should instill in young people a sense of values and norms which help them in adulthood to act, feel, and think in meaningful and constructive ways. This is, it should be noted, not the same as indoctrination. Indoctrination implies that a fixed set of moral, religious, or political doctrines and prejudices are imposed on people either by means of compelling propaganda or through sheer force. That is, in indoctrination the transference of values and norms to the young is basically undemocratic, since the mind and the will of the recipients are somehow stripped of their freedom and integrity. That is, of course, not at all what education is about.

Educational institutions, from primary school to university, are intrinsic components of civil society. It is only within a vital civil society and in conjunction with adjacent institutions, such as the family, the neighborhood, sports clubs, the church, and other associations, that this process of education can successfully instill a sense of values and norms in young people.

As to the university, scientific research is in itself, of course, free of normative value-judgments. That is, scientific research is in itself amoral. But neither the selection and conceptualization of problems to be investigated scientifically, nor the practical application of research findings are free of value-judgments and, in this sense, amoral. Moreover, although it is far removed from ideological indoctrination, scientific teaching does influence, if it is done well, the minds and souls of students morally. The scientific mentality, for instance, prevents people from an uncritical acceptance of facile, face-value statements, and make them sensitive to the need to avoid clichés and prejudices.

Apart from all this, if they are taught well, the sciences—the natural as well as the social sciences and the humanities—give its practitioners the joy of discovery and instills in them a never- ending curiosity as to the many things one does not yet know and understand. These are the primordial moral dimensions of the sciences and the humanities, and they are badly in need of rediscovery. Actually, they are being rediscovered in the present post-positivist and post-technocratic climate which to a certain extent was brought about by the waning of the comprehensive welfare state.

The Ideological Triangle and Its Aberrations

The Democratic Triangle—state, market, and civil society—is founded upon an Ideological Triangle which by and large covers the three predominant political currents that originated in Europe under the impact of the Enlightenment and the French Revolution: socialism (or social democracy as some prefer to call it), liberalism, and conservatism.[25] In the Anglo-Saxon world this triad is reduced to a dyad which finds its expression in a two-party system which covers the progressive-conservative continuum. As is well known, third parties have great difficulties in the Anglo-Saxon world establishing themselves in the political arena.

However, ever since the French Revolution the political spectrum of mainland Europe has been threefold (triadic) instead of twofold (dyadic). Surely enough in the process of modernization, and certainly in the context of the comprehensive welfare state, the three ideological movements—socialism, liberalism, and conservatism—have lost much of their idiosyncracies. Ideological differences have indeed become marginal nowadays. Yet, they have not disappeared, and with the rapid decline of the comprehensive welfare state, the three ideological movements seem to restore to a certain extent their original missions and distinct orientations.

Let us briefly reconstruct this Ideological Triangle. In its original orientation *socialism* or *social democracy* will focus primarily (not exclusively) on the state as the guardian of democracy, regulating and controlling the market and civil society. Equality is its main (not exclusive) value, followed by solidarity which is viewed first and foremost as class solidarity. Freedom or liberty is seen in socialism as a collective, not as an individual, moral property. It can only thrive in the context of equality and class solidarity. Socialist solidarity is not a matter of consensus but rather the result of conflict—the conflict of opposing class interests.

Liberalism in its classic eighteenth- and nineteenth-century expression puts prime emphasis on the market as the producer of the wealth that is needed to sustain democracy materially, and on the individual as the consumer of the market's products, searching rationally for the best products for the lowest prices (rational choice). The state is in the liberalist ideology an instrument for the realization and maintenance of a free market, but ought to be minimal, by all means not comprehensive and interventionist. Civil society is approached with care since it harbors scores of collectivities—organizations and institutions—which tend to minimize individual liberties and to obfuscate and therefore hamper efficient and effective decision-making processes. They are in the view of liberalism conservative obstacles to a smooth and efficient functioning of the market. From among the three values of the French Revolution—liberty, equality, and solidarity—liberalism is prone to emphasize primarily (and in many cases even exclusively) liberty or freedom which it views first and foremost as negative liberty in the market (free competition) and as positive freedom for individual citizens (political and civil rights). Equality and solidarity are the lesser of liberalist concerns. Equality is seen as an equality of chances, certainly not, as in socialism, as an equality of results. If consensual solidarity helps to expedite business, the true liberal will embrace it, but if the search for consensus rather slows down the decision making process, he will not hesitate to foster conflict.

Today classic liberalism is often identified with *conservatism* which is a grave mistake.[26] Conservatism's position within the Democratic Triangle is primarily (but not exclusively) in civil society compartment. True conservatives will emphasize the great importance of traditional collectivities—organizations and institutions—which constitute a meaningful order and function as civilizing mediating structures between the individual citizen and the potentially uncivil megastructures of the state and the market. With regard to the state, conservatives are usually inclined to position it in terms of subsidiarity: only the governmental and administrative issues lesser authorities are unable to deal with, are left to the state. As to the market, freedom of competition is acclaimed as long as it is not an unbridled and uncivilized, throat-cutting competition. Not so much the state, but organizations and institutions in civil society, often defined as corporations, like employers' associations and workers' unions (in Europe called "social partners"!), ought to guarantee an orderly market. Consensus, not conflict, is the dominant value of conservative policies. Solidarity is not based, as in socialism, on class consciousness but on a rather traditional, patrimonial kind of tolerance between culturally different status groups.

As the history of Western democracy has demonstrated, the Ideological Triangle has been perverted time and again. In fact, the Democratic Triangle is very vulnerable to such ideological aberrations, which are primarily caused by the radicalization of the ideological positions assumed within the triangle. In all three cases, democracy is being destroyed.

Perverse radicalization of socialism, for instance, leads to dictatorial *communism* which in the end always yields an unbridled, bureaucratized etatism that paralyzes both the market and civil society. In communism the prime socialist value of equality is altered perversely into a dreary and often violent egalitarianism, solidarity changes likewise into paranoid group control, whereas freedom or liberty is trampled upon ruthlessly. It is, of course, the end of democracy.

But liberalism too knows its own perversion when it is severed from the Democratic Triangle and radicalized into ideological isolation. Its aberration is *libertarianism* which eventually may end up in violent and irrational attacks on both the state and civil society. Anarchist assassinations in the past, perpetrated upon politicians, heads of state, or industrialists, are examples of such extreme libertarian actions, but so is the recent Oklahoma bombing, which was allegedly executed by a politically sectarian group. Such politically sectarian groups are often erroneously labeled as belonging to the "extreme right." They are, rather, radically libertarian and anarchistic.[27]

Incidentally, much of present-day postmodernism comes close to radical, libertarian liberalism in its recurrent attack on, or rather ironic derision of, the basic values of the Enlightenment. Like the romantics at the end of the nineteenth century, many postmodernists reject the rationalities of the state, the market and civil society. They hail in an anti-institutional and semi-anarchic manner fragmentation, individualization, relativization, and similar processes which undermine the very foundations of the Democratic Triangle. Needless to say, postmodernists embrace the Immoralist Ethos despite the fact that its structural *Sitz im Leben*, namely the comprehensive welfare state, has disappeared.

Finally conservatism too can and has been perverted by its own radicalization. Its focus on mediating organizations and institutions, as the backbone of civil society and the guarantee of a consensual order has, of course, a strongly corporatist bent. But as history has demonstrated such corporatism can easily degenerate into *reactionary fascism*. Indeed, if conservativism radicalizes its position at the expense of the delicate balance of the Democratic Triangle, it will easily fall prey to extremely right-wing, anti-democratic fascism, as has happened in Europe in the 1930s and 1940s, and is happening again in the reemergence of so-called radical-right movements. Usually, this fascist aberration of conservatism expresses itself in reactionary forms of nationalism and racism. Xenophobic hatred and resentment push the basic democratic values of equality, liberty, and solidarity ruthlessly aside.

A dark side effect of these ideological aberrations is the historically demonstrable fact that the three of them may easily coalesce and fortify each other. For example, during and after the political, socioeconomic, and cultural turmoil of the fateful Weimar Republic people from different ideological angles fell for the lures of Nazism. In fact, German national-socialism was initially an ideological cauldron of perverted socialism, liberalism, and conservatism. What kept the movement together was its antidemocratic, blood thirsty, and racist hatred and resentment.

There is no need to be pessimistic about the strength and perpetuation of the Democratic Triangle in Europe in the near future. But we should not be naive either. Since the heyday of the comprehensive welfare state which after all did offer a measure of material security, and since the days of the cold war which at least did draw some clear lines of political demarcation, are over, Europe has entered a very new phase in its development. If we also add the remarkable technological (electronic) revolution which is rapidly progressing in most European societies, and which affect the state, the market, and civil society deeply, we may draw the conclusion that this continent is once more at the crossroads: either it will drift away in a sea of uncertainty and insecurity, which will foster antidemocratic acts and sentiments, or it will strengthen the Democratic Triangle, balance its ideological impulses, and thereby fortify the many possibilities and challenges it still has in store. The maintenance and further solidification of a balanced Democratic Triangle is not just a political task. It is as much, or even more so, a moral task.

Conclusion

One of the culturally debilitating aspects of the comprehensive welfare state has been its tendency to neutralize moral considerations, to numb the moral veins of the people who conduct their everyday lives within its predominantly functional-rational, bureaucratic frame of reference. The combination of affluence and security easily pushed this moral neutrality in the direction of the immoralist type of ethos.

When the comprehensive welfare state was still at its zenith, it was an insult to be called a moralist. It suggested that this person lived in the past, in the "morally oppressive" 1950s. A moralist was an unworldly conservative, someone opposed to emancipation, dreaming of a world passed decades ago. It was meanwhile forgotten that morality—the sense of basic values and norms providing life with a meaningful direction— is the essence of the human condition, that without it human existence is driven to the abyss of anomie where civilization ends and men confront men like wolves. The Holocaust, Pol Pot's Cambodia, and recently the genocidal wars in Bosnia and Rwanda are bloody examples of a world without morality, drawn into the abyss of anomie. It is preposterous to derogatorily label someone who holds on to the fundamental fact of human morality, "a moralist." By the way, within the orbit of the social sciences where this derogatory accusation is often made, an alleged moralist is in good company. He knows profound thinkers such as Smith, Durkheim, and Weber are on his side.

But, it bears repeating that there was a strange paradox at work here. Beyond this immoralist type of ethos and its often latent cynicism strongly fostered by the comprehensive welfare state, many were simultaneously driven by an abstract kind of moralism which focused on miseries elsewhere in the world. Schelsky, we saw before, spoke of a "borrowed misery" located in the Third World due to a lack of misery in the affluent world. Gehlen, we also saw, even dubbed this global solidarity "hyper-morality." This hypertrophied brand of moralism was expressed in an emotionally heavy kind of ethic which Weber would have called the ethic of ultimate ends. In the 1960s and 1970s one could encounter such hyperbolic, rather abstract kinds of moralism in so-called new social movements like feminism and environmentalism. Feminist gurus like Betty Friedan unleashed a veritable "war over the family"[28] in 1963,[29] while in 1972 the Club of Rome set the apocalyptic tone for future environmentalists by its famous and influential report on the limits of economic growth. Wagner's *Götterdämmerung* was child's play compared to the global doom this elevated club of industrialists and academics had in store for us.

All this was accompanied in Europe by an emotionally tone-set socialism voiced by the likes of Alva Myrdal, Crosland, Wedgwood Benn, Brandt, Palme, and others whose fame and notoriety were great at the time but are fading these days rapidly. Like the fellow travelers of the 1920s and 1930s who adulated the still young Soviet Union, many European left-of-center intellectuals and artists in the 1960s and 1970s eulogized communist leaders in remote countries, such as Mao Tse-tung in the People's Republic of China, Fidel Castro in Cuba and Ho Chi Minh in Vietnam. There were critics, even in the left-of-center ranks, who kept their heads and hearts cool, mainly because they remembered the infamous days of the Moscow trials in the 1930s. But they were decried loudly. Anti-left critics were often called names like "capitalist lackeys," "reactionaries," and in a few instances even "fascists."

This is history now. It has become obvious once again that the worldly gods that had been pursued irrationally, have failed miserably. In fact, all that is left of Castro is a pathetic custodian of a ramshackle economy, a backward society, and insular culture. It is to be expected that some time in the future Ho Chi Minh City will be named Saigon again. After all even Leningrad's pre-communist name has been restored!

In sum, whatever else the waning of the comprehensive welfare state has brought about, it certainly has led to a resurgence of moral considerations which are founded upon a more down-to-earth and sober ethic of responsibility rather than upon an overexcited and at times delirious ethic of ultimate ends. It is, needless to add, the mentality and mind-set needed for the preservation and consolidation of a balanced Democratic Triangle resting upon an equally balanced Ideological Triangle.

Notes

1. These are, of course, *ideal types*, i.e., stenographic concepts which refer to highly complex realities. Naturally, "the" market, "the" state, or "the" civil society does not exist.
2. It is indicative that Adam Smith's *The Theory of Moral Sentiments* (Oxford: Oxford University Press [1759]1976; reprint by Liberty Fund, Indianapolis, 1984) draws much attention of economists and philosophers these days. The book remained largely unnoticed in the heyday of the comprehensive welfare state.
3. Francis Fukuyama, *Trust: The Social Virtues and the Creation of Prosperity* (New York: The Free Press,1995).
4. James S. Coleman, "Social Capital in the Creation of Human Capital," *American Journal of Sociology*, vol. 94 (1988), pp. 95–120.
5. See John A. Hall, G. John Ikenberry, *The State* (Minneapolis: University of Minnesota Press, 1989).
6. See Anthony D. Smith, *National Identity* (Reno, Nevada: University of Nevada Press, 1991).
7. Jean-Marie Guéhenno, *La Fin de la Démocratie*, (Paris: Editions Flammiron, 1994).
8. Cf. Manuel Castells, *The Rise of the Network Society* (Malden, MA: Blackwell Publishers, 1996).
9. This radically postmodernist view on the state was argued in depth by the Dutch scholar of public policy Paul Frissen in *De virtuele staat* ("The Virtual State"), (Schoonhoven: Academic Services, 1996).
10. Caroline de Gruyter, "De militairen verliezen hun zelfrespect" (Soldiers begin to lose their self-respect) *NRC Handelsblad*, 9 September 1995. The interviewed scholar is Martin van Creveld. It is curious for a historian to forget the history of the Weimar Republic in which due to the lack of a strong state, scores of armed bands, so-called *Freikorpsen*, roamed around and terrorized the civilians of those days.
11. See my monograph *A Theory of Urbanity: The Economic and Civic Culture of Cities* (New Brunswick, NJ: Transaction Publishers, 1998).
12. See W. F. Wertheim, "Society as a Composite of Conflicting Value Systems," in his *East-West Parallels* (Chicago: Quadrangle Books, 1965), pp. 23–38.
13. City of Rotterdam, *Nieuw Rotterdam: Cen opdrachsaan alle rotterdammers* (New Rotterdam: an Assignment to all Rotterdammers), (Rotterdam: Printer Tripiti, 1987).
14. City of Rotterdam, *Her-Nieurve Rotterdam in social Perspective.* (The New Rotterdam in Social Perspective), (Rotterdam: Printer Tripiti, 1989).
15. The related observations and policy advises of Jane Jacobs are still relevant and adequate: Jane Jacobs, *The Death and Life of Great American Cities* (New York: Vintage Books, 1961), in particular pp. 29–142.
16. Niklas Luhmann constructed a theory in which he defined procedures as the core of legitimacy. See his *Legitimation durch Verfahren* (Legitimacy through procedure), (Neuwied: Luchterhand, 1969).
17. As was remarked before, if there were any deregulation on the part of national welfare states, there was an exponentially increased regulation by the European Union in Brussels. There is much debate on this issue in today's Europe, particularly since it is generally believed that the democratic control of the European Commission by the European Parliament is wanting.

18. The economic problems of modern art, in particular its progressive alienation from the paying and buying public, is discussed by Arnold Gehlen, *Zeit-Bilder: Zur Soziologie und Ästhetik der modernen Malerei* (Time-Pictures: Towards a Sociology and Aesthetics of Modern Art) , (Frankfurt am Main: Vittorio Klostermann, [[1960]1986), in particular pp., 210–15.

19. See Jerzy Neyman (ed.), *The Heritage of Copernicus: Theories "Pleasing to the Mind,"* (Cambridge, MA: The MIT Press, 1974).

20. Giambattista Vico, *On the Study Methods of Our Time*, translated and introduced by Elio Gianturco (Indianapolis: The Bobbs-Merrill Company; The Library of Liberal Arts, [1709]1965).

21. A concise and helpful synopsis of Humboldt's idea of *Bildung* is given by Helmuth Schelsky, *Einsamkeit und Freiheit* (Loneliness and Freedom), (Hamburg: Rowohlt, 1963), in particular pp. 79–130.

22. Henry Adams, *The Education of Henry Adams* (New York: Random House; The Modern Library, [1907]n.d.).

23. Cf. Alvin W. Gouldner, *The Future of Intellectuals and the Rise of the New Class* (New York: Continuum, 1979).

24. Hansfried Kellner, Frank W. Heuberger, (eds.), *The Hidden Technocrats* (New Brunswick, NJ: Transaction Publishers, 1992).

25. I was inspired by J.W. de Beus et al. (eds.), *De ideologische driehoek: Nederlandse politiek in historisch perspectief* (The Ideological Triangle: Dutch Politics in Historical Perspective). (Amsterdam: Boom Meppel, 1989).

26. See Friedrich von Hayek's insightful exposition in which he explains why he is a liberal and not a conservative: "Postscript: Why I Am Not A Conservative," in F.A. Hayek, *The Constitution of Liberty*, (London: Routledge and Kegan Paul, 1960), pp. 397–414.

27. Anarchism is, of course, a multifaceted phenomenon. In its radicalized, libertarian form the freedom of the individual is absolutized to such an extent that all authorities are rejected and fought. An exemplary case has been Alexander Berkman (1870–1936) who was born in Vilna, Lithuania and came to New York when he was nineteen years old. Here he joined a radically anarchist group centered around Emma Goldman (1869–1940) and Johann Most (1846–1906). In 1892 he tried to assassinate the steel magnate Henry Clay Frick in his office for which he spent fourteen years in jail. His *Prison Memoirs of an Anarchist*, 1912, give a rare insight in the often warped mind and moods of a libertarian radical. Berkman was deported to Russia in 1917, disagreed (of course) with Bolshevism, roamed around through Europe and committed suicide in 1936 in Nice. The assassination attempt is described by Frick's biographer. See George Harvey, *Henry Clay Frick. The Man* (New York: privately printed by the Frick Collection, 1936), pp. 135–9.

28. See Brigitte Berger, Peter L. Berger, *The War over the Family*, (Garden City, NY: Anchor Press/Doubleday, 1983).

29. Betty Friedan, *The Feminine Mystique* (New York: Norton, 1963).

6

Conclusion

American readers may wonder what the relevance of the previous analyses and considerations might possibly be for them. The discussion was about an un-American, namely intensive and extensive (comprehensive) type of welfare state. This welfare state was then first analyzed as the result of a rather long, typically European history of state interventions as to the welfare and well-being of citizens (chapter 1). It was next described as a project which from the start has been characterized by ambiguities (chapter 2). Then the focus was on the remarkable confluence of an increasingly "value-free," amoral technocracy of the comprehensive welfare state on the one hand and a peculiar type of ethos, drenched in immoralism, on the other (chapter 3). The interventionist welfare state was above all a system which in most Western-European countries experienced after World War II a relatively short period of comprehensiveness (1960s and 1970s). It declined again after 1980 (chapter 4). Finally, a normative argument was set up to defend the so-called Democratic Triangle (state, market, civil society), undergirded by three ideologies (socialism, liberalism, conservatism), in view of possible inbalances due to the overemphasis and one-sided radicalization of one of the three components of the triangle. It was argued also that morality plays a crucial part in this necessary balance (chapter 5).

American readers will be struck, I think, primarily by two features of most European welfare states: first, their comprehensiveness, which entailed an at times excessively interventionist "etatism" that affected the market as well as civil society negatively; second, the ease with which most Europeans have accepted the encroachments of the state— its bureaucracy, its civil servants, and the state-supported professionals—upon their lives. However, as I tried to demonstrate, the days of the comprehensive welfare state are over. Even countries like Sweden and the Netherlands which have been prime examples of very intensive and extensive welfare states, have gone through a rather rapid and profound transformation—a process that is still going on and will continue to change the state, the market, and civil society of these countries in the near future.

An important question then is whether these Western European countries will become more "American" socioeconomically and culturally now that the days of the comprehensive welfare state, which apart from a few states never existed in the United States, are over. Some Europeans reject this idea and are inclined to follow analysts who claim lasting differences between the European and the American model of social policy. The European model will allegedly be less radical in the reduction of the role of the state than the American model. Whereas Americans, in this view, dismantle whatever has been left of the welfare state, Europeans will maintain a lean and mean welfare state as a statutory insurance against injustice, inequality, and socioeconomic misery. Apart from the often annoying gnostic dualism of the "good and just" model versus the "bad and unjust" model, such gross comparisons are generally useless. There are great historical and cultural differences between the various European countries, as there are considerable differences among the various states of America, certainly as far as welfare policies and provisions are concerned.

But if one would venture to generalize grandly, one would have to admit, I am inclined to conclude, that most post-welfare state countries in Europe will become more 'American' in their social policies. That is, there will be more room for voluntary initiatives, including charities and informal philantropies. Likewise, the ethic of ultimate ends will retreat and leave more room again for the ethic of responsibility. Since social rights are no longer taken-for-granted entitlements that allegedly complete the development of citizenship, most citizens will become responsible again for their own social security and welfare, let alone for their material and spiritual well-being. Only those who are guiltlessly indigent and in need of succor will be entitled to statutory assistance, while in addition the informal assistance of friends, neighbors, and family members will not be counted out beforehand anymore.

In the same generalizing vein one could also venture to conclude that morality and in conjunction with it civil religion will occupy a greater place in the mind and actions of most Europeans than was the case in the days of the comprehensive welfare state when the immoralist ethos and a penetrating secularism were the predominant factors in society. Also in this respect Europe will resemble America more than it did before, certainly if one takes into account that American morality and civil religion has lost much of its former strength and vigor in recent decades.[1] In this respect Europe is not only approaching America, the latter has come closer to Europe as well.[2]

Taking all this into consideration, the American reader who tries to understand the European welfare state—its origins, its comprehensiveness, and its waning—may want to hold on to the following propositions which were discussed and elaborated in this book.

First, the welfare state is neither the product nor the exclusive project of socialism, or left-of-center policies. In fact, conservatism has been an influential factor in its ascendance, as in the case of Bismarck who through statutory social arrangements tried to circumvent proletarian radicalism, or in the case of Roman Catholic social policy in the wake of the papal bull *Rerum Novarum* (1891). From the three basic democratic ideologies only liberalism has been seriously at odds with the welfare state. During the reign of the radical welfare state its influence and political importance was strongly reduced. The waning of the comprehensive welfare state meant the strong regeneration of liberalism, not only in politics but also in economics. The days of Keynes are over!

Second, "etatism" with its bureaucratic control and professional dominance is endemic to the comprehensive welfare state. It tends to curb free initiatives, creative inventions and experiments on the part of citizens in civil society. There is also the strong tendency to bridle the competitive forces in the market and to subject it to scores of rules and regulations. However, it would be very wrong to identify this with the state totalitarianism of communism or fascism, because in a welfare state set-up the state is recurrently called upon by the market and civil society to intervene in their affairs by means of tax benefits and scores of state subsidies to which, of course, rules and controls are attached. After all, who pays the piper chooses the tune! Moreover, unlike totalitarianism welfare "etatism" leaves abundant room for individualism, the pursuit of private interests and scores of civil and moral liberties. Needless to add that the welfare state never professed to kill capitalism. On the contrary, it maintained the capitalist mode of production, albeit in a Keynesian, state-controled manner. It has been called a "mixed economy."

Third, the welfare state is in its very origins a product of the Enlightenment and carries as such the moral ideals of this bourgeois movement. It represents the admittedly grand ideal of combining the two values of equality and liberty which are essentially contradictory, because if one tries to foster equality one will have to curb liberty as happens in socialism, while if one, on the contrary, wants to promote liberty, one is bound to create inequality, as in the case of liberalism. This fundamental ambiguity must be borne by the third value of bourgeois society, solidarity. It was believed initially and, as we know now, erroneously that the whole system would be embraced by the citizens in an emotional manner.

That did not happen. Soon enough the welfare state grew into an overbureaucratized, excessively interventionist megastructure in which the values of equality, solidarity, and liberty obscured progressively. After all, the welfare state is to all intents and purposes a "value-free," amoral, rather technocratic megastructure, experienced by citizens as a meddling system of redistribution, not as something to bear and share in feelings of solidarity. But it is precisely this abstract and functional-rational megastructure which promoted, as in an elective affinity, the ethos of immoralism expressed in an emotional, substantial-irrational ethic of ultimate ends.

Fourth, not surprisinly ambiguity is the hallmark of the comprehensive welfare state. A morally crucial ambiguity is the legal one. Statutory assistance needs, of course, in a democratic *Rechtsstaat* legal coverage. As a result, there was a huge overproduction of social legislation in the comprehensive welfare state. Dutch social legislation has been correctly called a jungle of rules, regulations, and controls in which only a few experts know their way. One of the perverse effects has been that improper use of welfare benefits could occur massively, while at the same time many people in need were ignorant of the welfare benefits to which they were entitled. In addition, many subsidies, as in the world of the arts, where seats in theatres and concert halls were (and actually still are) subsidized by the state, served mainly the well-to-do middle-class. In sum, the whole system was legal but its legality was very weakly undergirded by legitimacy.

Fifth, much talk about the "crisis of the welfare state" focused on the economic fact that the system led, as in an almost autonomous development, to enormous overspending and in some cases to astronomic public deficits. Deregulation, decentralization and privatization—the basic components of the shrinking of the comprehensive welfare state—were propagated first and foremost as instruments to curb public spending. But it was also pointed out that the comprehensive welfare state suffered from a kind of administrative elephantiasis which in terms of public policy was exceedingly cumbersome. In the end the ever-expanding state bureaucracies were inefficient and ineffective, their rationality irrational, their legality illegitimate. Obviously, management was not well developed in the public sector as a whole.

Social scientists failed in general to point out the negative effects the comprehensive welfare state had upon civil society. They were, in fact, the main, predominantly left-of-center ideologues of the welfare state which rewarded them for this loyalty with a lavish funding of their research. Meanwhile, it became abundantly clear that civil society began to suffer under the welfare state's regime, particularly because of the progressive loss of autonomy on the part of its organizations and institutions. They developed gradually into extension pieces of the ever more centralized state. In fact, they surrendered themselves to the state, its rules and regulations, its civil servants and professionals in exchange for subsidizing and funding largesse.

Sixth, by the end of the 1970s and the beginning of the 1980s it had become clear to all parties involved that the comprehensive welfare state could no longer be sustained economically, politically, socially and culturally. Some countries like Great Britain and the Netherlands started in the early 1980s with this major transformation, others like Sweden changed the course of their welfare states later. But going into the 1990s it was clear that the days of the comprehensive welfare state were over in Europe.

Next to these internal factors, there have been external factors at work which prompted the radical change of the European welfare states. These external factors were (a) the two oil crises in the 1970s which demonstrated painfully how dependable and vulnerable Western European nations were in terms of their economies; (b) the sudden collapse of the Soviet Union, the end of the cold war, and the ensuing reunification of Europe which prompted a radical reorientation of international political and economic relations; (c) the growing political and economic interdependence within the European Union and its emphasis on regions and cities rather than on nation-states; (d) spectacular developments in the electronic media (fax, the Internet, e-mail) which had strongly decentralizing effects and which rendered traditional borders and limits increasingly porous.

Seventh, the waning of the comprehensive welfare state brought into the picture again the overarching importance of a balanced Democratic Triangle. The state, the market and civil society, ideologically supported by socialism (or social democracy), liberalism and conservatism, ought to remain in mutual balance. In particular the fundamental moral missions of these three foundations of democracy ought to be reformulated and reinstalled again now that the intensive and extensive welfare state is passing away.

The state has to be reestablished as the *Rechtsstaat*; that is, the constitutional state which bears prime responsibility for the defense of fundamental human rights and guarantees order and safety—not as the bureaucratic distributor of benefits and the legalistic, yet hardly legitimate defensor of social rights and entitlements which supposedly were the copestone of citizenship but in the end reduced citizens to welfare dependents. But this constitutional state will not allow vulnerable and socioeconomically defenseless people to drift away into economic, social, and cultural misery. In that respect the constitutional state must continue to function as a welfare state.

The market should be reestablished again as the main motor of our material prosperity and must therefore be liberated from scores of encroachments upon its freedom of competition by the state. Yet, the market ought to function also as the proper environment in which business can be conducted, to quote Michael Novak, "as a morally serious calling."[3] The market cannot and should not try to generate moral sentiments but is itself not an amoral phenomenon. It could simply not function well without basic virtues like honesty, work ethic, mutual trust, and fair play.

Finally, civil society ought to be reevaluated as the main well of all morality, as the feeding and breeding grounds of human values, norms, and meanings which can only prosper in a context of autonomous and self-regulating associations (organizations and institutions) functioning as morally powerful intermediary structures.

Eighth, as however the often tragic history of Europe has demonstrated time and again, it is exceedingly difficult to maintain a balanced democracy. Its three fundamental ideologies have in the past often enough degenerated into radically antidemocratic movements. The collapse of the Soviet Imperium which had kept Central and Eastern Europe under a debilitating, iron-fisted control and tutelage, opened for these liberated societies the road to a market economy and a democratic polity. But the voids that the communists left in what should be a civil society, were often filled with atavistic forms of nationalism and racism, and with corruption and organized crime. Something similar occurs in the seams of Western European societies where neo-fascist, ultra-right movements appeal to the sense of insecurity and xenophobia on the part of those who have most to lose in the post-welfare state society.

The waning of the comprehensive welfare state has been an internally and externally necessary and unavoidable process. The near future will demonstrate if Europe will manage to establish and maintain a viable and properly balanced Democratic Triangle. As most member states of the European Union demonstrate, there are sufficient reasons to face Europe's future with confidence. However, as the Atlantic Partners they are ever since World War II, both, Americans and Europeans, ought to heed in conjunction the three ideological aberrations—communism, libertarianism, and fascism. They have always lurked behind the scenes in Europe, and brooded under the surfaces of this rich and fateful continent.

The waning of the comprehensive welfare state in Europe which entails the restoration of the Democratic Triangle is a process of transformation which carries many risks and insecurities. But it will in the end strengthen Europe's political, economic, and sociocultural stamina. If it also draws the Atlantic Partners closer together, as I believe it does, the chances of another European communist, libertarian, or fascist *Götterdämmerung* will remain remote.

Notes

1. See Robert N. Bellah, *The Broken Convenant: American Civil Religion in Time of Trial* (Chicago: University of Chicago Press, [1975]1992); and Robert D. Putnam, "Bowling Alone" *Journal of Democracy*, 6 Dec. 1995, pp. 65–78.
2. An argument can definitely be made also for a "Europeanization" of America. It is apparent, for instance, in the attempts to develop and revitalize urban downtowns, for which European cities are often used as examples. But also in life style and consumption patterns European influences are notable. In the American upper middle-class, to give just one simple example, a "wine culture" has emerged which, as I recall, was still absent in the mid 60s.
3. Michael Novak, *Business as a Calling* (New York: The Free Press, 1996), in particular chapter three: "A Morally Serious Calling," pp. 54–77.

Index